Supporting Students in a Time
of Core Standards

NCTE Editorial Board

Supporting Students in a Time of Core Standards

English Language Arts, Grades 3–5

Jeff Williams
Solon City Schools, Ohio

with
Elizabeth C. Homan
The University of Michigan

Sarah Swofford
The University of Michigan

NCTE National Council of Teachers of English
1111 W. Kenyon Road, Urbana, Illinois 61801-1096

Staff Editor: BONNY GRAHAM
Manuscript Editor: THERESA KAY
Interior Design: JENNY JENSEN GREENLEAF
Cover Design: PAT MAYER
Cover Background: ISTOCKPHOTO.COM/ARTIOM MUHACIOV

NCTE Stock Number: 49416

Library of Congress Cataloging-in-Publication Data

Williams, Jeff.
   Supporting students in a time of core standards : English language arts, grades 3–5 / Jeff Williams with Elizabeth C. Homan, Sarah Swofford.
        p. cm.
   Includes bibliographical references.
   ISBN 978-0-8141-4941-6 (pbk)
   1. Language arts (Elementary)--United States--States. 2. Education, Elementary--Standards--United States--States. I. Homan, Elizabeth C. II. Swofford, Sarah. III. Title.
   LB1576.W48845 2011
   372.4--dc23

                                                                                                    2011038516

Contents

Acknowledgments

Collaborating with Elizabeth Homan and Sarah Swofford has been an immense pleasure. I am thankful for their time, efforts, and organizational skills and for their willingness to put up with me. I am equally grateful to Anne Gere for pairing me with such an adept team; I am indebted to Anne for her vision in organizing the series and for her thoughtful comments and editing along the way.

This book would not have been possible without the incredible teachers who are showcased within—the vignettes captured in this book reflect a tiny fraction of the talent and professionalism that each teacher represents. I am grateful to Jalynn Clayton, Scott Hutchinson, Kelley Kyff, Erin Meyer, Dana O'Brien, and Katie Plesec for graciously sharing their craft, reflections, and understandings.

I am grateful to have had the opportunity to work with many fine members of NCTE and the Executive Committee and thank them for their dedication and principled leadership, especially my friends Kylene Beers, Barbara Cambridge, Keith Gilyard, Sandy Hayes, Carol Jago, and Kent Williamson.

I am deeply appreciative of the Solon City School District in Solon, Ohio, and for all the amazingly gifted and wonderfully dedicated people with whom I work. Particularly, I am indebted to Joe Regano and Debbie Siegel for their leadership and commitment to excellence; to my teacher-leader colleagues Sue Adams, Nancy Erkkila, Marcea Harrison, Dini Kwiatkowski, Cari Mineard, Denise Morgan, Katie Plesec, Barb Slaby, and Sabrina Tirpak for their thinking and talents; and to the many principals and teachers of Solon who inspire me to do my personal best every day.

I am thankful for the insights and thinking of many researchers and writers who have shaped my passions and understandings about literacy and teaching, including Richard Allington, Nancie Atwell, Kylene Beers, Lucy Calkins, Shirley Clarke, Marie Clay, Diane DeFord, Irene Fountas and Gay Su Pinnell, Ken and Yetta Goodman, Donald Graves, Stephanie Harvey and Anne Goudvis, Peter Johnston, Ellin Keene and Susan Zimmermann, Michael Pressley, Katie Wood Ray, Regie Routman, Margaret Searle, Frank Smith, and Constance Weaver.

And finally, without the encouragement and understanding of my family I would never have found the time or energy to complete this book. I am ever-thankful for my parents, Bobi and Gene Harris, for instilling in me their work ethic and understandings about life, and equally thankful for my best friend and partner, Will LaRiccia, for his patience, constant tech help, and unwavering support in all things.

I

Observing the CCSS

⊚ Introduction

Not long ago I was driving a van filled with middle school soccer players and heard a voice from the back say, "I hate, I hate, I hate the MEAP." (The MEAP is Michigan's state test of math and English language arts [ELA].) I recognized the voice as that of a friend of my daughter, a good student, diligent in every way. Her class had just spent a month preparing for and then taking the MEAP, and she was feeling frustrated by the time spent and anxious about her performance.

That plaintive voice reminded me of concerns I've heard expressed about the latest chapter in the standards movement. The appearance of the Common Core State Standards (CCSS) has aroused a variety of responses, some of them filled with anxiety and resentment. It's easy to get worried about issues of alignment, curricular shifts, and new forms of assessment. And it's frustrating, after carefully developing state ELA standards, to have to put them aside in favor of the CCSS. As one teacher put it, "The CCSS are less detailed than the standards they are replacing." Another lamented, "How are teachers supposed to have time to rewrite curriculum and realign lessons to CCSS now that the state has taken away our meeting times?"

Yet, responses to the CCSS have also been positive. Some teachers have said that the grade-specific standards are helpful because they provide useful details about learning goals for students. Others have noted that the CCSS can help them address the needs of transient students because teachers in different schools will be addressing similar learning goals. Still others have commented that the CCSS can provide a lens through which they can examine their own teaching practices. As one teacher put it, "Looking at the standards made me realize that I wasn't giving much attention to oral language." Another said, "I think they provide more opportunities for higher-order thinking and an authentic application of the content we teach."

Regardless of teacher responses, the CCSS are now part of the educational landscape. But these standards do not replace the principles that guide good teaching. Some things remain constant regardless of new mandates. One such principle is that teachers think first of their students, trying to understand their learning needs, developing effective ways to meet those needs, and continually affirming that the needs are being met. This book, like all four volumes in this series, is written with and by teachers who remain deeply committed to their students and their literacy learning. It is a book addressed to teachers like you. You may be an experienced teacher who has established ways of fostering literacy learning or you may be a relative newcomer to the classroom who is looking for ideas and strategies, but that you are holding this book in your hands says that you put students at the center of your teaching.

No one knows as much about your students as you do. You understand the community that surrounds the school and helps to shape their life experiences. You have some information about their families and may even know their parents or guardians personally. You can tell when they are having difficulty and when they are feeling successful. You have watched their body language, scanned their faces, listened to their voices, and read enough of their writing to have some ideas about what matters to them. Your knowledge about your students guides the instructional choices you make, and it shapes your response to any mandate, including the CCSS.

Your knowledge about students is probably connected to your knowledge of assessment. You know the importance of finding out what students have learned and what they still need to learn. You probably already know about the importance of authentic assessment, measures of learning that are connected with work students can be expected to do outside of class as well as in it. No doubt you use formative assessment, measures of learning that give students feedback rather than grades and help you know what they still need to learn. For example, you probably make sure that students respond to one another's written drafts as they develop a finished piece of writing. You may have individual conferences with student writers or offer marginal comments and suggestions on their drafts. Or perhaps you meet individually with students to hear them read aloud or tell you about what they have been reading. Whatever type of formative assessment you use, you probably use it to guide the decisions you make about teaching.

You may have read or heard about the principles for learning adopted by NCTE and other subject-matter associations, principles that position literacy at the heart of learning in all subjects, describe learning as social, affirm the value of learning about learning, urge the importance of assessing progress, emphasize new media, and see learning in a global context. These principles, like others articulated by NCTE, provide a North Star to guide instruction regardless of specific mandates, and you probably recognize that teaching based on such principles will foster student achievement, including achievement of the CCSS.

Because you are concerned about the learning of *all* of your students, you probably try to find ways to affirm the wide variety of racial, ethnic, socioeconomic, and religious backgrounds that students bring into the classroom. No doubt you are interested in taking multiple approaches to reading, writing, speaking and listening so that you can engage as many students as possible. Taking this stance convinces you that continual growth and innovation are essential to student achievement, especially when new standards are being introduced.

This book is designed to support you in meeting the challenges posed by the CCSS. It stands on the principle that standards do not mean standardization or a one-size-fits-all approach to teaching. It assumes that inspirational teaching—teaching that engages students as critical problem solvers who embrace multiple ways of representing knowledge—can address standards most effectively. It celebrates new visions of innovation and the renewal of long-held visions that may have become buried in the midst of day-to-day obligations. It reinforces a focus on student learning by demonstrating ways of addressing these standards while also adhering to NCTE principles of effective teaching. It does this by, first, examining the CCSS to identify key features and address some of the most common questions they raise. The second section of this book moves into the classrooms of individual teachers, offering snapshots of instruction and showing how teachers developed their practices across time. These classroom snapshots demonstrate ways to address learning goals included in the CCSS while simultaneously adhering to principles of good teaching articulated by NCTE. In addition to narratives of teaching, this section includes charts that show, quickly, how principles and standards can be aligned. Finally, this section offers suggestions for professional development, both for individuals and for teachers who participate in communities of practice. Thanks to NCTE's online resources, you can join in a community of practice that extends across local and state boundaries, enabling you to share ideas and strategies with colleagues from many parts of the country. Embedded throughout this section are student work samples and many other artifacts, and NCTE's online resources include many more materials, from which you can draw and to which you can contribute. The final section of this book recognizes that effective change requires long-term planning as well as collaboration among colleagues, and it offers strategies and materials for planning units of study articulating grade-level expectations and mapping yearlong instruction.

Voices in the back of your mind, like the "I hate, I hate" voice in the back of my van, may continue to express frustrations and anxieties about the CCSS, but I am confident that the teachers you will meet in this book along with the ideas and strategies offered will reinforce your view of yourself as a professional educator charged with making decisions about strategies and curriculum to advance the learning of your students.

Anne Ruggles Gere
Series Editor

Demystifying the Common Core State Standards

Some teachers are uncomfortable with standards because they assume that the use of standards implies a lack of understanding about the needs of children or that standards somehow erase teachers' creativity and professional judgment. And, dependent upon how you use them—if standards are seen only as a checklist of what to teach— then they could be right. However, if you view standards as common ending points that you hope to get students to and you understand that formative assessment tells you where all of your students' starting points are (including the reality that many children will come to you already past these standard endpoints), then the need for creative and professional judgments are actually more important and critical. Ultimately, my ability to move all students forward from where they start still comes down to my decisions about texts and experiences and my craft of teaching.

—Katie Plesec, K–4 Literacy Coach

Putting students at the center means thinking first about the kinds of learning experiences we want them to have, and since forty-plus states have adopted the Common Core State Standards (CCSS), many teachers will need to think about student learning in light of these standards. First, though, it will be helpful to understand where these standards came from and what they actually say.

The CCSS are part of a long-term movement toward greater accountability in education that stretches back to the early 1990s. In this line of thinking, accountability focuses on student achievement rather than, say, time spent in classrooms or materials used, and standards like the ones developed by states beginning in the 1990s have been used to indicate what students should achieve. Because of this emphasis, standards are often equated with educational transformation, as in "standards-based school reform." Proponents of standards-based reform have differing views of how standards should be used. Some assume that standards can lead to investments and curricular changes that will improve schools, while others see them as linked to testing that has little to do with allocating resources that will change schools for the better. This book operates from

Web 1.1
Throughout this volume, you will find links, reproducibles, interactive opportunities, and other online resources indicated by this icon. Go online to www.ncte.org/books/ supp-students-3-5 to take advantage of these materials.

the assumption that ELA teachers can use standards as a lens through which they can examine and improve the what and how of instruction, and the vignettes in Section II demonstrate how teachers are doing this.

The CCSS for English Language Arts and Mathematics, then, are the latest in a series of standards-based school reform initiatives. They were coordinated by the National Governors Association Center for Best Practices (NGA Center) and the Council of Chief State School Officers (CCSSO) to prepare US students for both college and the workplace. This partnership of state governors and state school superintendents worked with Achieve Inc., an education reform organization founded in 1996 and based in Washington, DC, to develop the CCSS. Funding for their work was provided by the Bill and Melinda Gates Foundation, the Charles Steward Mott Foundation, and other private groups. Each state decided whether to adopt the CCSS, and the US Department of Education created an incentive by linking adoption of the CCSS to Race to the Top (RTT), requiring states that applied for RTT funds to adopt the CCSS. When the CCSS were released in June of 2010, more than forty states had already agreed to adopt them.

In the states that have formally adopted them, the CCSS will replace state standards. States may add 15 percent to the standards, which means that some elements of state standards could be preserved or new standards could be developed. The full text of the ELA standards, along with other explanatory materials, is available online at http://www.corestandards.org/the-standards/english-language-arts-standards.

In September of 2010, two consortia of states, the Partnership for the Assessment of Readiness for College and Careers (PARCC) and the SMARTER Balanced Assessment Consortium, were funded—also with RTT monies—to develop assessments to accompany the CCSS, and these assessments are scheduled for implementation in 2014. At this point it is impossible to know precisely what the assessments will include, but preliminary documents indicate that formative assessment may play a role, that computers may be involved in both administration and scoring, and that some parts of the assessment, such as writing, may occur over multiple days.

Web 1.2

For updates on the development of CCSS assessments, check online.

I don't have time to read through the entire CCSS document, so can you give me a quick summary?

The ELA standards for grades K–5 address four basic strands for ELA: reading, writing, speaking and listening, and language. Although each is presented separately, the introduction to the CCSS in English Language Arts advocates for an integrated model of literacy in which all four dimensions are interwoven. In addition, the CCSS for grades 6–12 include standards for history/social studies and science and technical subjects, which

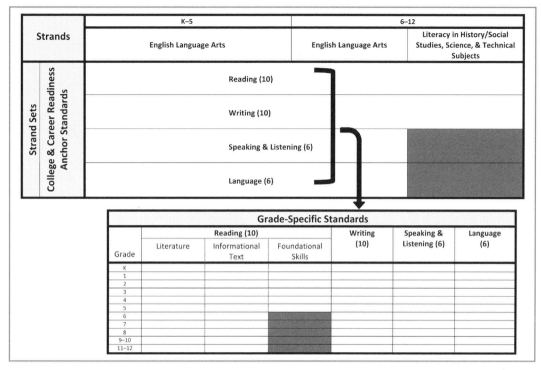

Strands		K–5		6–12	
		English Language Arts		English Language Arts	Literacy in History/Social Studies, Science, & Technical Subjects
Strand Sets	College & Career Readiness Anchor Standards	Reading (10)			
		Writing (10)			
		Speaking & Listening (6)			
		Language (6)			

	Grade-Specific Standards					
	Reading (10)			Writing (10)	Speaking & Listening (6)	Language (6)
Grade	Literature	Informational Text	Foundational Skills			
K						
1						
2						
3						
4						
5						
6						
7						
8						
9–10						
11–12						

FIGURE 1.1: Structural relationships of the CCSS.

have reading and writing strands. Each strand has overarching Anchor Standards, which are translated into grade-specific standards. Figure 1.1 shows the structural relationship of the two.

The content of the two is similarly linked. For example, the K–5 Anchor Standards for writing include the category "text types and purposes," and one of the Anchor Standards in this category reads: "Write arguments to support claims in an analysis of substantive topics or texts, using valid reasoning and relevant and sufficient evidence." The fourth-grade standard that addresses this Anchor Standard includes the following:

1. Write opinion pieces on topics or texts, supporting a point of view with reasons and information.

   a. Introduce a topic or text clearly, state an opinion, and create an organizational structure in which related ideas are grouped to support the writer's purpose.

b. Provide reasons that are supported by facts and details.

c. Link opinion and reasons using words and phrases (e.g., for instance, in order to, in addition).

d. Provide a concluding statement or section related to the opinion presented.

To see examples of how teachers implement these and other grade-specific standards in their classrooms, turn to Section II of this book.

Needless to say, the introduction of the CCSS raises many questions for teachers and other instructional leaders. New mandates such as the CCSS can generate misconceptions and even myths, so it is important to look at the standards themselves. Because the implementation of the CCSS is an ongoing process, and because assessment is still under development, the online community associated with this book provides updates as well as a place to share ideas and experiences.

Web 1.3

What's the relationship between the CCSS and the standards my state already developed?

There may well be some overlap between the CCSS and the standards developed by your state, particularly when you look at the more global goals of the Anchor Standards. Because it is possible to supplement the CCSS with up to 15 percent of state standards, some state standards may be preserved, but generally in states that have formally adopted the CCSS these new standards will replace existing state ones. The timing of implementing CCSS varies from one state to another, with some states shifting immediately and others doing it over a year or two.

There are some distinct differences between the CCSS and state standards:

- First, they are intended to be used by all states so that students across the United States will be expected to achieve similar goals, even though they may reach them by different routes.

- The interdisciplinary emphasis of including literacy standards for history, science, social studies, and technical subjects in grades 6–12 makes the CCSS different from most state ELA standards.

- The CCSS emphasize *rigor* and connect it with what is called *textual complexity*, a term that refers to levels of meaning, quantitative readability measures, and reader variables such as motivation and experience.

- The CCSS position students as increasingly independent learners, frequently describing tasks they should perform "without assistance."

Will the CCSS create a national curriculum?

No. The CCSS focus on results, on what students should know and be able to do rather than the specific means for achieving learning goals. As the introduction to the CCSS states on page 4, "the Standards leave room for teachers, curriculum developers and states to determine how these goals should be reached and what additional topics should be addressed. . . . Teachers are thus free to provide students with whatever tools and knowledge their professional judgment and experience identify as most helpful for meeting the goals set out in the Standards." In other words, the CCSS focus on what students should take away from schooling, but they stipulate that teachers should decide what to teach, how to teach it, and when and for how long to teach it. The CCSS acknowledge that teachers know what students bring to the classroom and how they learn best. Ongoing professional development, especially communities of learning with colleagues, will ensure that teachers have the content knowledge and expertise with instructional strategies to foster effective student learning.

I've heard that the CCSS include lists of *exemplar* texts. Isn't that going to create a national curriculum?

The CCSS do include lists of texts on page 58 that illustrate what is called text complexity for each grade-level band. At the 4–5 level, for instance, the texts include both literary and informational texts. Among the literary selections are *Alice's Adventures in Wonderland* by Lewis Carroll, "Casey at the Bat" by Ernest Lawrence Thayer, *The Black Stallion* by Walter Farley, "Zlateh the Goat" by Isaac Bashevis Singer, and *Where the Mountain Meets the Moon* by Grace Lin. Informational texts include *Discovering Mars: The Amazing Story of the Red Planet* by Melvin Berger; *Hurricanes: Earth's Mightiest Storms* by Patricia Lauber; *Freedom: A History of US* by Joy Hakim; *Horses* by Seymour Simon; and *Quest for the Tree Kangaroo: An Expedition to the Cloud Forest of New Guinea* by Sy Montgomery.

Web 1.4

However, these texts are simply offered as examples of topics and genres that teachers might include, not as specific texts to be adopted in all classrooms.

Teachers need to select texts appropriate for their own students and for the context in which they work. As the vignettes in Section II show, teachers can use a variety of texts to address the CCSS—Dorothy Sterling's *Freedom Train: The Story of Harriet Tubman* and Kate DiCamillo's *Because of Winn-Dixie* are just two of them. The vignettes also show that these central or fulcrum texts work best when surrounded by contextual and texture texts that add perspective and meaning. For example, *The Lightning Thief* by Rick Riordan, when used as a read-aloud text, takes on new dimensions when read alongside informational texts such as Ingri and Edgar D'Aulaire's *D'Aulaires' Book of Greek Myths* and accompanied by language study and journey narratives from contemporary society.

What more do we know about text complexity?

In Appendix A, page 4, the CCSS define text complexity as "level of meaning, structure, language conventionality and clarity, knowledge demands, word frequency, sentence length [all in the context of] student knowledge, motivation and interest." This definition is expanded in a three-part model—qualitative dimensions, quantitative dimensions, and reader and task considerations. The quantitative dimension refers to features, such as word length or frequency, sentence length, and cohesion, that can be calculated by computers. The qualitative dimension refers to levels of meaning, structure, language conventions, and knowledge demands that cannot be measured well by machines but require careful attention from experienced readers/teachers. The reader and task considerations in Appendix A, page 4 include student motivation, knowledge, and experience as well as the purpose for reading, again, features that can be discerned by teachers "employing their professional judgment, experience and knowledge of their students and the subject."

It is worth noting that the CCSS acknowledge the limitations of this model of text complexity, particularly for literary forms such as poetry. Quantitative measures, for example, simply don't provide useful information about the relative complexity of a poem. Nor do they provide a useful measure of the complexity of much narrative fiction. As the CCSS observe in Appendix A, page 8, "some widely used quantitative measures, including the Flesch-Kincaid Grade Level test and the Lexile Framework for Reading, rate the Pulitzer Prize–winning novel *Grapes of Wrath* as appropriate for grades 2–3." This means that teachers need to play a key role in deciding what constitutes textual complexity for their students.

What does *rigor* mean in this context?

Rigor is used in relation to text complexity. For example, in describing the reading standards for literature on pages 11 and 36, the CCSS include this sentence: "Rigor is also infused through the requirement that students read increasingly complex texts through the grades." Rigor refers to the goal of helping students to continue developing their capacities as readers so that with each passing year they build upon skills and understandings developed during the previous year.

Teachers who immerse their students in rich textual environments, require increasing amounts of reading, and help students choose ever more challenging texts will address rigor as it is defined by the CCSS. This means keeping students at the center, motivating them to continually develop as writers and readers, and engaging them in literacy projects that are relevant to their lives. When students feel personal connections, they are much more willing to wrestle with complex topics/texts/questions. Student engagement, then, offers the best route to rigor.

Will implementing the CCSS mean eliminating literature in favor of "informational texts"?

It is true that the CCSS give significant attention to nonfiction, and on page 5, the introduction includes this statement: "Fulfilling the standards . . . requires much greater attention to a specific category of informational text—literary nonfiction." According to the CCSS, the amount of nonfiction should be increased as students mature so that by the time they are seniors in high school 70 percent of their reading should be nonfiction. But it is also true that the CCSS describe literacy development as a responsibility to be shared by teachers across multiple disciplines, so this doesn't mean that 70 percent of reading in ELA classes should be nonfiction. The standards for history/social studies, science, and technological subjects demonstrate how responsibility for reading nonfiction should be spread across multiple courses.

To reinforce this point, on page 5, the CCSS introduction underscores the importance of teaching literature: "Because the ELA classroom must focus on literature (stories, drama, and poetry) as well as literary nonfiction, a great deal of informational reading . . . must take place in other classes." The CCSS advocate the combination of adding more nonfiction to the curriculum in history/social studies, science, and technical subjects along with including more nonfiction in ELA. This combination still leaves plenty of space for literature in ELA studies.

Do the CCSS advocate separating reading, writing, speaking, listening, and language from one another?

No. Although the standards are listed separately, the CCSS propose an integrated model of literacy. On page 4, the introduction explains, "Although the Standards are divided into Reading, Writing, Speaking and Listening, and Language strands for conceptual clarity, the processes of communication are closely connected, as reflected throughout this document. For example, Writing standard 9 requires that students be able to write about what they read." This integrated approach fits well with NCTE principles and with the ELA standards developed by many states.

Formative evaluation is becoming increasingly important in my school. How do the CCSS address this?

Since the assessment portion of the CCSS is currently under development, it is impossible to know how it will address formative evaluation. The preliminary descriptions offered by the PARCC consortium use the phrase "through course components," which is described as "actionable data that teachers can use to plan and adjust instruction." This suggests that formative evaluation could well be part of the CCSS assessment.

This could be good news because formative evaluation is assessment *for* learning, not assessment *of* learning. When assessment helps teachers understand where students are having difficulty, as well as where they understand clearly, it is possible to adjust instruction to address the areas of difficulty. Research shows that formative assessment can be a powerful means of improving achievement, particularly for students who typically don't do well in school.

Because assessments for the CCSS will be under development until 2014, it is worthwhile to monitor and perhaps contribute to their evolving shape.

Web 1.5

The websites for PARCC and SMARTER Balanced each include a list of the "governing states," and once you have determined which consortium your state is participating in, you can get in touch with the state representative(s) to learn more.

What do the CCSS say about English language learners and/or students with special needs?

In a section titled "What Is Not Covered by the Standards" on page 6, the CCSS explain, "It is also beyond the scope of the Standards to define the full range of supports appropriate for English language learners and for students with special needs. At the same time, all students must have the opportunity to learn and meet the same high standards if they are to access the knowledge and skills necessary in their post–high school lives." This section goes on to say, "Each grade will include students who are still acquiring English. For those students, it is possible to meet the standards in reading, writing, speaking and listening without displaying native-like control of conventions and vocabulary." Based on this, we might assume some flexibility in applying the CCSS to English language learners.

The statement on page 6 about students with special needs takes a similar position: "The Standards should also be read as allowing for the widest possible range of students to participate fully from the outset and as permitting appropriate accommodations to ensure maximum participation of students with special education needs." Clearly the CCSS provide only limited guidance for implementing the standards with English language learners and students with special needs.

Am I wrong to think that the CCSS will undercut teacher authority?

Probably. The CCSS make frequent reference to teachers' professional judgment and emphasize that teachers and other instructional leaders should be making many of the crucial decisions about student learning. The implementation of the CCSS by individual states and/or school districts could have negative consequences for teachers, and it is impossible to know what will result from the as-yet-undeveloped assessment of the CCSS.

Still, in the best case, the CCSS can offer benefits to teachers. They can make it easier for teachers to deal with transient students by assuring that they have been working toward similar goals in their previous school. The CCSS can provide a lens through which teachers can examine their own practice to find areas that would benefit from more instructional attention or to introduce more balance into the curriculum. A number of teachers have reported that state standards had such effects, and it is reasonable to think that the CCSS might function similarly. Most of all, the CCSS can provide an occasion for teachers to consider what constitutes the most effective ELA teaching.

What is NCTE's stake in the CCSS?

Although it commented on drafts of the CCSS when they were under development, NCTE did not participate in creating these standards. As an association most directly concerned with professional development, NCTE is invested in supporting teachers as they face the challenges posed by the CCSS. In addition, it is an association that values teacher voices, like the ones included in Section II of this volume. To that end, the Executive Committee of NCTE commissioned and invested in the four-volume set to which this book belongs. NCTE is also devoting online resources to providing materials that extend beyond this book and provide a space where communities of teachers can share ideas and strategies.

How should I begin to deal with the CCSS?

As the introduction to this book suggests, it makes sense to begin with students because teachers know more about their students than anyone else. As a first step you might make a list of goals for the students you are teaching now. Consider the skills, dispositions, motivations, habits, and abilities you would like them to develop. Your list probably encompasses every standard in the CCSS along with a good deal more. Keep your entire list in mind as you approach the CCSS, and start by thinking about what your students need to learn.

Looking at the learning needs of students in light of the CCSS can lead, in turn, to considering classroom practices and thinking about how various instructional strategies might be refined or adapted to foster student learning. Looking at classroom practices leads to questions about instructional materials and, ultimately, the curriculum. Woven through all of these is the continuing theme of professional growth and development because asking questions and reconsidering nearly always require changes that are best supported by professional development.

The Common Core State Standards (CCSS) may feel like yet another set of top-down, mandated standards. And integrating the CCSS into the curricula and teaching can, at times, generate feelings of pressure and conflict. But it is also possible to approach the CCSS from a different perspective as well—one that sees opportunities for bridging between good practice based on NCTE principles and policy and what the CCSS offer. The NCTE community, of which this book series is a part, is one space where you can start to build bridges and frame your interactions with the CCSS in ways that are empowering, highlight and encourage best practices in literacy learning, and sustain the incredible work that English teachers are already doing in classrooms. Rather than focusing on how the CCSS will subvert the instruction we are already doing, framing our approach to the standards instead around observing, contextualizing, and building can help us to bridge the CCSS and established instructional practices based on NCTE principles, allowing the two to work in tandem.

First, one way to frame discussions about and approaches to the CCSS is to focus on detailed observation. Before we can become teachers who incorporate these standards in meaningful and pedagogically sound ways into our practices, we need to be learners who observe and take careful note of what exists in the document and what the standards are asking of students. We also need to develop observational lenses through which to see the standards that will keep students and their needs at the center of all instructional change. Learning about the CCSS through close observation may better equip us to advocate for our students' unique needs.

A second way to think about the standards is to use them as a frame for contextualizing. It is important to remember that, while we observe and take note of what exists in the CCSS document itself, we always need to keep specific school and classroom cultures and environments in mind, understanding how different teaching contexts can pose different challenges and opportunities. The teaching vignettes you will read in Section II seek to display and honor a variety of school contexts, cultures, and teaching environments, but not all of the teachers in this volume approach planning with the CCSS in the same way, and their lessons don't look the same. A consideration of local context, then, must be coupled with detailed observation of the CCSS document itself.

Third, we can see the CCSS as a frame for building our instruction and classrooms and for meeting students where they are and keeping their needs at the center of lesson design and instruction. To build with the CCSS in mind, we need to begin to see them as more than boxes to check off on a list or forces mandated from above that are seeking to destroy our classrooms. Instead, building *from* and at times *with* the CCSS will involve developing knowledge about the document itself, examining and evaluating our current experiences in the classroom and the culture in which we teach, and relying on the communities around us for support and assistance.

This book, then, is framed around observing the CCSS closely, contextualizing these standards to address specific students in specific schools, and building instruction that integrates the CCSS with NCTE principles for teaching English language arts.

Observing

Detailed observation of the CCSS can begin with identifying where the standards may present shifts from previous state standards documents and identifying patterns in the language of the CCSS document. By looking across the document in this way, you can see some of the most salient shifts. Below, you will find a brief overview of student-focused shifts and instructional shifts that occur in the CCSS document, as well as references to specific CCSS document pages where you can seek greater specificity about these themes.

Student-Focused Shifts

- *Meaning-making*—The CCSS require that students will do more than just read texts for basic comprehension; instead, students will be expected to pull from multiple sources to synthesize diverse texts and ideas, consider multiple points of view, and read across texts. (See, for example, pages 8 and 40 of the CCSS document.)

- *Developing independence*—The ultimate goal of each standard is that all students will demonstrate the ability to enact key skills and strategies articulated in the CCSS on their own. To help students reach this goal, the CCSS spiral expectations across grade levels. Standards for the elementary grades, for example, include language about how students should enact the standard "with support." To clarify, this expectation does not diminish the need to scaffold instruction at all grade levels; rather, the goal is to move students toward independent enactment of standards. (See the CCSS document, page 7. Note that while there are times when the language of independence is explicitly stated, as on page 55, this expectation is also embedded in assumptions about all CCSS.)

- *Transfer of learning*—On page 7, the CCSS state that students will be required to respond to a variety of literacy demands within their content area courses—ELA *and* others—and to discuss with others how their ability to meet these demands will prepare them for the demands they will face in college and in their future careers.

- *College and career readiness*—Linked to transfer, on page 7, the CCSS expectations articulate a rationale for what college- and career-ready high school students will be able to do. There is little, if any, focus on rote memorization. Rather, the CCSS focus is on skills, strategies, and habits that will enable students to adapt to the rhetorical demands of their future learning and contributions.

Instructional Shifts

It is important to reiterate that the CCSS do not mandate *how* teachers should teach; this is even stated explicitly on page 6 in the document. Why a focus on instructional shifts? Clearly, just as the CCSS spell out what students will be expected to do, the CCSS may prompt shifts in our thinking about how best to help students meet these expectations, which will inevitably affect our teaching.

- *Spiraling instruction*—Unlike some state and district standards, the CCSS do not promote instructional coverage. Instead, the CCSS invite spiraled instruction. Students will be expected to enact particular standards repeatedly within grade-level content area courses *and* across grade levels. In part, this is evident when tracing the lineage of a particular standard to the grade level below and above. Parts of particular CCSS are repeated and built on in subsequent grades. The CCSS are therefore meant to build iteratively. On page 30 of the CCSS document there is a graphic representation of this spiraling idea with regard to language skills, but a similar graphic could just as well be created to illustrate the approach to the other ELA threads as well. For further discussion of spiraling instruction, see Section III of this volume.

- *Integration of ELA threads*—On pages 4 and 47, the CCSS encourage an "integrated model of literacy" whereby ELA threads (e.g., reading and writing) are woven throughout units of study.

- *Inclusion of nonfiction or informational texts*—On page 5, the CCSS set explicit expectations regarding the kinds of texts students read and write. By twelfth grade, 70 percent of the sum of students' reading, for example, is to be informational, nonfiction reading. But as we discuss further in Section III, the responsibility for this reading is shared by all content area teachers. Still, the inclusion of more informational text may present a shift for some.

- *Text complexity*—Page 57 of the CCSS document offers a descriptive graphic on text complexity. NCTE principles affirm the range of ways that strong ELA teachers introduce increasingly complex texts to student readers. These include but are not limited to student interest, genre, language, content, and ELA concepts foregrounded in instruction.

II

Contextualizing

Reading Deeply: Themes and Ideas within Rich Texts

2

Meet Jeff Williams, K–12 Literacy Coach and Reading Recovery Teacher, Solon, Ohio

In this section of the book, you will be introduced to six teachers who work with grades 3–5 students in their classrooms every day. We will learn more about their teaching and how they integrate the CCSS into their instruction. Through their experiences, perhaps you will learn more about framing the CCSS in your context and find some useful ways to build on curriculum that already affects student learning. We will read how these teachers continue to make learning come alive for their students and, at the same time, face the challenges that often accompany integrating a new set of standards.

In my twenty-one years of being an educator, I have had many roles and experiences: I was a classroom teacher for ten years, a Reading Recovery teacher, a literacy coach, an author, an adjunct professor supporting and teaching new teachers, and a literacy consultant in more than forty districts across the country. Throughout these varied experiences, though, I have learned several lasting principles that continue to shape my thinking and my work: the importance of teacher knowledge and reflection, the impact of formative assessment and responsive teaching, the power of gradual release and scaffolding, and the effects of collaboration. Regardless of the challenges created by changes in policy, resources, student needs, etc., I find that solutions come to us through some magical combination of these principles. Naturally, then, I rely on these principles as we begin to work in the time of Common Core State Standards.

Our first endeavors with the new standards must involve teachers deepening their content knowledge about the specifics of the standards. In the district where I work, this process has already begun with teacher teams identifying what is already known and understood by them and what areas are likely to need more study and thought. Here we see great promise in most of the standards and how they are designed to allow for depth, and here we question the relevance or necessity of other standards. Before we embark on the journey of actually teaching, we are drawing conclusions about where energies need to be spent. Deepening our knowledge of the content is only one component of our learning; we are simultaneously engaged in growing our expertise with pedagogy—understanding the conditions for learning and working to develop such conditions for all students is ever present in our discussions.

As part of our work in the coming years, we will follow a process that has served us well in the past—considering what needs to be taught (the standards) together with how we know to best help students achieve and grow through gradual release and scaffolding. Again, teacher teams work collaboratively to design instruction, creating or finding resources that will best fit the needs of their students. These plans always include aspects of formative assessment both to determine what the majority of students need in the form of whole-group instruction and what individuals need within guided or individual instruction. Formative assessment also helps to calibrate our effectiveness when we stop to reflect on how students are learning along the way and then adjust accordingly.

Throughout the process, collaboration is the central mechanism that helps us deepen our knowledge through collective sharing about our understandings and experiences. Collaboration is paramount in creating the classroom cultures and structures that allow us to differentiate instruction to meet the needs of students effectively and efficiently. We are fully aware that there exists no one resource where all needs can be met, so we work to create our own resources that are continually revised, reorganized, and refined dependent on current needs. Collaboration also allows us to expand our knowledge of how to scaffold appropriately for different learners and enables us to share our knowledge of books, resources, and techniques, and language that supports learning is ongoing and embedded in our day-to-day operations.

As you can see, it is not just one of these principles that is the key but rather the unique combinations that allow for professional development and personal growth. Teachers teaching one another and being open to opportunities for growth and the hard work that this requires is what true professionalism entails.

Beyond my experiences, I see this same passion and professionalism across many contexts and present here some of the stories of these teachers to share with you. Each teacher vignette represented in this volume has aspects of these principles (and more), and I hope that you are as inspired by their experiences as I am.

Each vignette is preceded by a brief description of the context in which the teacher and his or her students are working, and the vignette is followed by an explanation of the teacher's journey because, as we all know, exemplary moments in teaching are the product of many years of studying classroom practice, discussing ideas with colleagues, and reflecting on teaching and learning. Charts following vignettes highlight some of the teaching practices, connecting them with specific standards in the CCSS and with NCTE principles. Footnotes point toward research that supports the teaching described here.

The online component of this book offers additional classroom vignettes along with questions to prompt reflection and generate conversations among readers who want to deepen their understanding of their students and expand their professional knowledge of literacy theory and practice.

Contextualizing

The way we design instruction with local context and the CCSS in mind determines the kind of learning that will emerge on the canvas of our classrooms. What we emphasize, what we say, and what we spend our time engaged in will emerge in what and how our students learn. So, we are deliberate, knowing that what happens on the first day and how it connects to the last day matters. We are precise, cognizant that the language of learning permeating our classrooms affects thinking.

It is our hope that these teaching and learning vignettes and the corresponding materials will serve as a reflection of the language of learning that already fills your classrooms, and that they will demonstrate a framework that allows thinking about not just *what* we do, but *why* we do it. We hope they will remind us that in the layers of local, state, and national values, the greatest intentionality comes from the classroom teacher who enters the complexity and emerges with a process that honors the learning in our classrooms. We invite you to step into these classrooms, reflect on them, and use their successes and challenges to further your own thinking about what bridges you can build between the CCSS and your own instruction.

As you read through the chapters in this volume, look for the following symbols to signal various themes and practices.

 Common Core State Standards

 **Collaboration**

 Connections

 **Integrated Teaching and Learning**

 Honoring Diversity

When looking across the CCSS documents, it is apparent that deep reading of text is valued above surface reading for literal information. This shift is welcome but in many cases warrants more study and consideration. If students are required to read more deeply, what are the qualities of texts that will allow for this kind of reading? Though some short texts are in fact built with the ability to be read deeply, most are not. Reading deeply will require more focus on longer texts with embedded elements throughout that require readers to sift and sort information, question and infer understandings, and weigh and measure words. In the following

 Connections
Section III focuses exclusively on the building frame. There, you will find specific resources for building your instruction with the CCSS and for working with colleagues to observe patterns in the CCSS document compared to previous local and state standards.

sections, you will meet two teachers who are adept at choosing quality children's literature, using it through a variety of settings, to help their students do this kind of deep reading.

Meet Katie Plesec, Parkside Elementary School

Katie Plesec is an energetic and thoughtful fourth-grade teacher in a suburban public school in Solon, Ohio. She began her teaching career in Solon in 1999 and has recently become a literacy coach and curriculum specialist where she shares her passion and knowledge of language arts teaching with district colleagues. Katie teaches and coaches at one of the four elementary schools in the district.

The Solon City Schools, located near Cleveland, Ohio, have 5,100 students that represent a diverse population with 31 percent of the student population being African American, Hispanic, Asian or Pacific Islander, or multiracial. Currently, Solon serves double the state average of English language learners and, as with many school districts across the country, the number of English language learners and economically disadvantaged students in Solon continues to grow. Based on factors related to state achievement tests, such as meeting AYP goals with all groups in all subjects and grade levels, Solon is consistently ranked to be one of the top three school districts out of the 611 districts in Ohio.

A typical K–4 classroom in Solon has twenty-four students that represent Solon's diversity equally. Special education students are served through an inclusion model by a special education teacher who is in the room daily for language arts. All K–6 teachers have 120 minutes of language arts taught through a Reading and Writing Workshop approach, with K–4 teachers being self-contained for all subjects. To emphasize the importance of literacy, *all* of Solon's fifth- and sixth-grade teachers teach their own language arts block and then students are rotated into the other content areas of math, science, and social studies.

Who Needs What? Katie's Classroom

Katie uses formative assessments at the beginning of each quarter to determine the needs of her students in relation to standards. Teams of teachers analyze their grade-level performance on these common assessments to determine what kind of instruction and how much instruction students need on given topics from the curriculum.

With this in mind, they collaboratively plan mini-lessons and guided reading sessions to address the needs of all students, differentiating to support these students within the workshop approach.

Katie identifies that many of her students need a deeper understanding of author themes, and she works to create meaningful experiences with identifying and supporting these themes for her students. Through a series of mini-lessons that span a week, Katie models and explains the concept of theme and engages her students using many formative assessment techniques such as turn-and-talk partners, Popsicle sticks, and ABCD cards. Toward the end of a mini-lesson, Katie poses a multiple-choice question about the theme of a book she has read aloud to her students. Students hold a set of 3" × 5" cards in their laps, each with a letter—A, B, C, or D—written on it, and Katie asks students to choose the best answer and then flash the letter on the count of three. Using this strategy, Katie is able to determine in only a few seconds that the majority of her students have flashed the letter B, the answer which is most correct, which tells her that her students understand the concept. Because getting correct answers is not the only goal of this activity, Katie chooses from a jar of Popsicle sticks, each with a student's name written on it, to randomly call on students to share their thinking about the process they went through to choose a certain answer. Katie also demonstrates, by thinking aloud, why answer C was close but did not express the main theme of the text.

Honoring Diversity

Teachers with learning technologies such as SMART Boards could use polls in the same way Katie uses ABCD cards. Such techniques also engage students in sharing the thinking that went into how they arrived at an answer and helps to demonstrate that there are often multiple ways of understanding.

Each day after the mini-lesson, Katie's students either read independently or meet with her in a small guided reading group of four to six students. Students who are reading independently are asked to respond weekly to a question that usually pertains to their current focus of instruction, which in this case is theme. In guided reading (Biddulph, 2002; Fountas & Pinnell, 1996, 2001, 2006), Katie works with students to guide them toward deeper application of theme in a meaningful context using authentic literature of a sufficient challenge for each group.

One of Katie's groups (which contains students who have had the most difficulty with this concept) is reading the novel *Because of Winn-Dixie*, by Kate DiCamillo, and they are near the end of the book. Katie selected this text knowing that it contains rich language and multiple opportunities for students to notice and note themes with her support and guidance. Katie asked the group in a previous guided reading session to locate a place in the text where they think they have identified a theme. Each student comes prepared with not only a theme but also vigorous support for the theme they have chosen. As Katie listens to the following exchange, she records anecdotal notes to document

Common Core State Standards

The standards place a lot of emphasis on theme and require that students be able to use evidence from texts to support their claims; here, Katie addresses both of these requirements by guiding her students with scaffolded questions.

student thinking about the learning focus of theme and uses the student exchange to scaffold learning:

KATIE: Arrika, did you have something that you wanted to say?

ARRIKA: Um, on page 159, when Opal and Gloria was looking for Winn-Dixie . . . how um, Gloria says, "There ain't no way to hold on to something that wants to go. You understand? You gotta love what you got while you got it." And I thought that was a theme.

KATIE: I think that's a huge piece, Arrika, that you just tapped into. Reread that, guys, and think about it.

Arrika reads aloud the paragraph where her evidence is located. As she does, another student visibly has an aha moment and says quietly, "Oh!"

KATIE: What else could that be talking about?

EMMA: Like about her mom, 'cause when she left . . . and she wants to try to find her. But, um, Opal is trying to find her and she's saying you only have what you got.

KATIE: How do you see that as the lesson, Arrika?

ARRIKA: 'Cause when someone goes, you have to move on. You can't just keep thinking about it.

KATIE: So, what I'm hearing, Arrika, is that you're seeing a theme, and I'm going to use just one word to sum it up [writes the word *acceptance* on the white-board], but I see you saying you see a theme of acceptance in the book . . . you kind of have to accept what happens. . . .

EMMA: Yeah, accept what you have. . . .

KATIE: . . . and love what you have when you have it but understand that some-times things change and you can't control that.

ARRIKA: Yeah.

KATIE: [turns to other students] Do you think that is possibly a theme in this book? [Students nod yes.] Did you have the same theme?

EMMA: No, I had a different one.

KATIE: Okay, let's look at a different one because I think there are multiple themes in the book, but really nice job, Arrika, of giving us that piece of text to support what you thought the theme was.

Each student goes on to give and support, with evidence from the text, other themes such as the importance of family relationships/love and of friendships.

At the end of her guided reading session, Katie has ample evidence that this group of students understands the concept and can apply the concept in their reading. Another group of students who demonstrated a good understanding of theme in the mini-lessons and formative assessments early on are working with Connie, the special education teacher. Both teachers recognize the need to stay deeply connected to students at all levels; they often switch roles, working with students at all ability levels within the classroom. As Connie works with more proficient students, she also engages the readers in her group by requiring them, with her guidance, to go beyond identifying and talking about themes. She uses some of the small-group time to teach students how to write an extended paragraph about themes with support from the text, helping them to synthesize concepts learned in the mini-lesson with ideas they glean from the example text itself.

Honoring Diversity
Some teachers may not have the ability to engage multiple adults in work with smaller groups. However, teachers can still provide this differentiated learning environment through the choice of different texts for different learning/reading abilities or through the incorporation of different activities—such as the synthesis paragraph Connie does here—for different groups of students.

Because Katie feels confident that her students are able to find and discuss themes, as a final reflection, Katie uses an "exit slip" to ask her students to reflect metacognitively on what they now understand about theme and how knowing this will help them as readers. With these student reflections, what she has observed and recorded during the performance assessment setting of guided reading, and her use of exit slips and other formative assessment data (Clarke, 2001), Katie makes further instructional decisions regarding whether students understand this concept and are ready for more or whether she needs to teach in ways that will deepen or extend student learning.

Katie's Journey: Pathways to Enact These Practices

As Katie reflects on her eleven years with the Solon City Schools, she concludes that her career has been shaped largely by in-district forces—particularly by the strong, collaborative professional learning community and the instructional leaders in her district. Katie feels that the ongoing learning opportunities offered by the district literacy teacher leader had great impact on the shape of her reading and writing workshops. Additionally, her curriculum director has been and still is a tremendous influence because she constantly challenges Katie to be innovative and intentional with her work. In addition to her district resources, Katie also relies heavily on professional readings, with *Language Arts* and *Educational Leadership* being two publications that have helped her over the years, both as a classroom teacher and as an instructional coach.

Collaboration
The support systems in place at Katie's school challenge her to continue reflecting and transforming her teaching. Consider what motivates you to do the same or who you might collaborate with at your school to accomplish similar goals.

As a teacher and literacy coach, Katie is continually reflective about many aspects of her teaching: she sets professional goals for herself and reflects on her progress toward them; she anticipates the needs of the students or adults that she works with and reflects on her approach toward helping them grow; and she considers research and her own new learning, thinking of possibilities for incorporating them into her work.

Literacy assessment is one particular area about which Katie is deeply reflective. When asked if the types of assessments used now are different from when she first started teaching, and how assessment has changed for her across her career, she smiles and nods. When she first began teaching, the assessments were comprehensive and were given to assess student learning at the end of a learning cycle. Today, there are many different ways that she assesses learning, with more of them being formative—short, focused assessments used to measure learning during the learning cycle so that teaching can be adjusted as needed. These assessments vary in format but all serve the same idea—to help Katie determine how well students are learning concepts and to assist her in planning next steps. She does rely on a few more comprehensive summative assessments, which are used periodically to measure how students are retaining learning, but these are still given with the purpose of planning instruction. As her district has embraced formative assessment, Katie has learned firsthand about the power of this type of assessment. She now sees students being much more successful on the summative assessments because she has used formative assessments to adapt instruction along the way.

As mentioned earlier, Katie is part of several deeply involved professional learning communities in Solon. Her district has scheduled time into each day for teacher collaboration—time for teachers to analyze data and/or plan instruction. Katie considers the work done in her professional learning communities to have immense power in shaping her as a teacher and a learner: "This collaboration is the only way to fulfill our district mission of helping each student succeed. We need to collaboratively develop our best instruction and share our strategies for reaching all students. This certainly helps us as teachers, but students really benefit because instead of one teacher being responsible for their learning, it's all teachers on the team sharing responsibility. This collective responsibility and accountability ensures all students get what they need to be successful."

Meet Scott Hutchinson, McKean Elementary School

Scott Hutchinson's classroom is vibrant with the activities of fourth-grade students busily interacting with one another during a discussion period at McKean Elementary School, part of the General McLane School District, located in western Pennsylvania. This rural district of 2,100 students has a demographic profile like many rural districts throughout the country—lower numbers (4 percent) of

African American, Hispanic, and Asian students; typical numbers (13 percent) of special education students; and larger numbers (25 percent) of students from low-income families. Scott's building has approximately 10 percent more low-income students than the entire district average.

Scott works diligently to ensure that his students are meaningfully engaged and that they are well-prepared to go to the next grade level. He uses technology thought-fully and builds community around shared experiences and knows that engagement is paramount to learning. Scott has established classroom routines and structures that allow students to share thinking with one another in focused ways and use technol-ogy to extend classroom conversations beyond the school walls and day. This vignette exemplifies one way that Scott uses his expertise to teach students about the language and structures of fiction and demonstrates how he creates understandings that go beyond standards to create readers and thinkers.

Using Technology to Enhance Learning: Scott's Classroom

Scott plans collaboratively with teammates to develop units of study for reading—he and his colleagues use a series of lessons centered on a concept in reading or writing that is built using the gradual release of responsibility model (Pearson & Gallagher, 1983), wherein the concept is modeled first and then shifts toward guided or shared experiences, until finally students can apply the learning independently. One such unit developed in Scott's grade level is about theme.

At the beginning of the unit, Scott models the interactive read-aloud process for his students. Scott has identified many "mentor texts" for this unit, texts that have many examples of the concept that he is currently teaching to demonstrate the concept and texts to be used for guided prac-tice. Some texts are used repeatedly for different purposes across a school year, which allows the children's attention to go toward new or deeper understandings about a literary element such as theme. At the beginning of the unit, Scott reads aloud from *The Fabled Fourth Graders of Aesop Elementary School* by Candace Fleming because the book has qualities that engage and delight readers and because each chapter happens to have a particular theme or life message. By thinking aloud for students, Scott demonstrates not only what theme is but also how a reader goes about noticing themes that can be stated directly by the author or that can be inferred by readers.

> **Integrated Teaching and Learning**
> Because children in Scott's classroom are involved directly in providing some of the language for these charts, interaction with and reference to these charts is frequent. Often, the charts can be added to or amended over time as new understandings about the concept develop. Lists of examples from read-aloud or independent reading are often helpful touchstones that remind students of concrete experiences they have had with the concept.

After a day or two of this, Scott begins to shift toward shared/guided practice by inviting students to work collaboratively in what he calls "RW Partners"—designated student pairings who know to sit close to one another for the purpose of think/pair/share or turn-and-talk opportunities. Using this predictable routine affords Scott ample time for student collaboration, because time is not wasted finding a partner or in getting to the task. During the read-aloud, Scott periodically stops and poses a question or statement for pairs to discuss quickly and then share out with others. Scott has taken time early in the year to build a reading/writing community that uses "grand conversations" (Eeds & Wells, 1989), specifically teaching students how to share their thinking with others, how to disagree without judgment, and how to add into a conversation. Because these routines and structures are employed early and consistently, Scott is able to maximize time in his classroom for these important interactions around complex concepts.

Another form of shared/guided practice is the use of a classroom blog to continue conversations about the concept at home. Scott uses a free format called School Fusion Classroom, which provides some unique features ideal for the elementary classroom. The site is secure, private to students, and free from advertisements. One beneficial feature is that students are randomly assigned the name of a color and animal, like Red Cheetah, each time they post or add comments to the posts of others. This anonymity for students (although the teacher's version shows real student names) eliminates issues of competition, popularity, and/or reluctance to participate due to shyness or learning differences. Another feature allows students to give others awards for the quality of their comments, for example, a Visionary Award for insightful posts or a Scholar Award for informative posts. On one such blog, Scott is able to see how his students are beginning to get the idea of theme represented in his read-aloud from *Chicken Soup for the Teen Soul* (see Figure 2.1). In this example, Scott quickly notes that his students are appropriately talking about theme and that they are supporting and challenging one another.

Honoring Diversity

For teachers with students who cannot easily access the Internet at home, teachers could use class time to engage students in "blogging" as Scott does here. If access to computers is limited, teachers could consider asking students to journal their thoughts on theme and share their journals with others. Students could do this anonymously by not including their names on their journals.

Scott also requires students to use sticky notes in their independent reading books to capture thinking about themes. He routinely meets with small groups of students or with individuals to check on and confirm their understandings of theme, offering feedback, guidance, or corrective instruction as necessary. By recording anecdotal notes and collecting artifacts of student thinking, Scott gains useful insight into the understandings of his students. He also reflects on his own practices—questioning and refining his teaching moves, examples, and use of gradual release. Scott and his teammates debrief and share with one another any new understandings they have as teachers about theme in general or about the design of their unit of study so that adjustments to future teaching can be made.

Scott's Journey: Pathways to Enact These Practices

Scott's teaching career actually began in high school when he realized as a ski instructor that he loved "teaching others how to become successful

> **Carrot Chinchilla:** I think that the theme is not to lie because if you lie you just get in big trouble then you just have to make up other lie to get out of it.
>
> >**Pacific Alligator:** I agree with you because I had to make up all kinds of lies to get out of one
>
> >>**Midnight Marten:** i agree with u, but i want to add on. I think that if u lie someone is going to get in trouble and that is going to be the person that lies
>
> >**Shadow Fox:** I think the theme is a blend of not to lye and don't do something you don't know about because Franciso said that his grandpa knew about gardening but he didn't know so that led to lying.
>
> >>**Forest Chameleon:** I agree with u because that totally makes sence
>
> >>**Brick Bat:** Grandpa didn't lie though!
>
> >>**Desert Deer:** I DISAGREE with you because, I don't think that you can blend.
>
> >>**Desert Deer:** What to mean?
>
> >>**Brick Bat:** I think the theme is that honesty is the more important than knowing how to do things.

FIGURE 2.1: An excerpt from students' blogs about theme in Scott's classroom.

at something." After finishing college, Scott found himself teaching first grade, where he says he learned a valuable lesson from a colleague who influenced him toward adopting the stance that "whatever is best for kids is the avenue that reaches the most kids."

When Scott began teaching fourth grade in his present school district, he relied heavily on the teaching manuals that were available to him—partly out of being new to the grade level and partly out of comfort in doing what he thought was necessary. As time went on, Scott began to question some of his practices and reflected on the results he was dissatisfied with as a teacher. His district encouraged him to read professionally and to have dialogue with colleagues regularly. In doing so, Scott was exposed to the thinking of Irene Fountas and Gay Su Pinnell, who led him to a reading workshop approach that, in turn, helped to foster a genuine "joy of reading for kids." The work of Lucy Calkins has also influenced Scott in the realm of writing instruction—helping him to deepen his own knowledge of writing and writing workshop and, at the same time, helping him to instill a love of writing in his students that complements their love of reading. From these valuable resources, Scott says he went "from teaching based on manuals to teaching based on need." In his regular collaboration with colleagues, Scott felt empowered and believes that "my own school district was a strong factor in teaching me that my opinion counts."

Connections

Scott finds ways to connect with teachers in online communities and also conducts his own research to improve his practice; for ideas about resources connected to grades 3–5 reading instruction, see Appendix A. For more information on ways to connect with professionals outside your school, see Section III.

Scott was also influenced by finding other teachers on the Internet who were willing to share their creative ideas with others. "I talk with teachers in other schools as well as teachers within my school, regardless of the grade level. Experienced teachers who hold the same values as I do about kids should always be appreciated and utilized for their ideas." Listening to and sharing with other teachers have had a positive effect on Scott: "My methods of instruction and classroom environment are always changing. I utilize the experiences of other teachers to open my mind to all options and to help guide my decisions." Because of this openness to ideas, Scott feels his students "get the most meaningful instruction and the most productive and enjoyable work environment possible."

As Scott's views of teaching have shifted, so has his view of assessment. Instead of testing children's abilities solely at the end of a cycle of learning, in a unit test or piece of writing, Scott is more comfortable with and reliant on various formative assessments. "I think I simply assess more now than I ever did. My assessments are every day—whether that be in my observations of students' sticky notes, or anecdotal notes I've written about a student during a reading conference or as part of guided reading—these assessments guide my daily instruction. Assessments never guided me as frequently as they do now." When asked why he thinks his view on assessment has shifted, Scott adds, "It is all about teaching based on the needs of the students, not the schedule of my lesson plans. My assessments guide me and assess me as a teacher, compared to being solely about creating a grade for a student."

> **Integrated Teaching and Learning**
>
> Scott changed his approach to assessment when he saw the benefits of frequent formative assessment for his students; his reflective approach to his teaching led him to reconsider his approach and employ more low-stakes, formative assessment in his day-to-day instruction.

Scott's journey is like that of many teachers—one of questioning and searching for answers, being open to new ideas, and of making decisions based foremost on the needs of students. "I have developed confidence in my teaching and in my ability to back up my choices. It is interesting that, at the same time, I really never have total confidence that I am doing everything I could be doing; I think that pushes me to always desire to grow as a teacher."

Charting the Practices

As Katie and Scott illustrate, how we think and talk about learning speaks volumes about what we value. The teachers in these vignettes jointly value fostering students' lifelong learning and their development as readers and writers. As we illuminate a range of pathways by which teachers plan with this goal in mind, we would be negligent if we represented planning as a recipe with the same steps for all. In fact, our individual planning processes vary widely across time, courses, and students. Figure 2.2 represents the range of pathways, or processes, by which

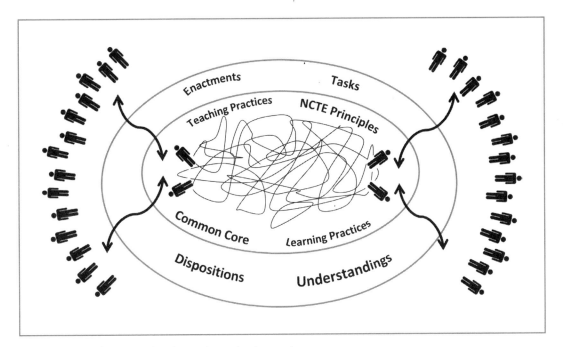

FIGURE 2.2: Pathways to planning and enacting instruction.

teachers consider the integration of their teaching and the learning they plan for students.

Through reflection or conversation, the teachers in these vignettes speak to some form of wrestling with chaos in describing their thinking about planning. Figure 2.2 represents the chaos that we all navigate, but it also seeks to honor the fact that how we enter this chaos—the pathways by which we get there—varies. Some teachers enter through knowledge about their students, which are represented in the figure as encompassing and informing our thinking. Some teachers enter by thinking about the ultimate goals they have for their students; these are represented in the language of the outer circle including the dispositions, understandings, tasks, and enactments teachers expect students to demonstrate or develop. No matter the entrance, once in the middle we ultimately navigate the chaos that involves considering importantly the meeting place and relationship between these goals and the CCSS, NCTE principles, our teaching practices, and the learning practices we personally develop as well as those we foster in our students. The narratives offered by Katie and Scott affirm that we meet these considerations through various pathways differently over time.

Figure 2.2 visually represents the way we conceptualize these inextricably linked considerations that are at the heart of our decision making as teachers. We intentionally chose not to represent them as linear, and one of our earliest versions of this figure actually included the words in the inner circle embedded within the chaos of the nest at the middle. Given the difficulty of actually reading this chaos, we chose in favor of readability; however, the original visual may more accurately represent why at times it is difficult for us to articulate the complexity of our thinking, acting, and ongoing learning about how to work with and meet the needs of diverse learners. Still, we believe it is possible and quite critical that we work to identify our decision making as well as how we conceive of the elements that inform our decisions, especially as we remind ourselves and others that even as we prepare students to meet their standards, the CCSS do not dictate the path we choose.

We hope that you will keep Figure 2.2 in mind as you read the charts that follow and that you will find at the end of each vignette chapter. In these charts, we endeavor to represent how the instructional decisions that emerge out of the chaos are dynamic. For ease of representation, these charts read more linearly than the processes they depict. But they include the elements of our decision making and moving out of the chaos toward deliberate goals and outcomes. Therefore, our movement toward the CCSS is informed by the NCTE principles about what makes for strong ELA instruction and learning. With these principles in mind, we enact teaching practices that invite students to enact learning practices that will enable them to meet the CCSS. The relationship between teaching and learning practices is key. Our teaching opens the space and makes explicit for students how they can learn to enact particular tasks and to ultimately take on particular dispositions toward lifelong learning.

Therefore, the charts below highlight some of the key NCTE principles about and teaching practices for reading instruction that the teachers in this chapter's vignettes enact, connecting these to specific Reading Anchor Standards in the CCSS document, and merging how teachers expect students to evidence their ability to enact the standards in their learning.

Common Core State Standards That This Practice Supports

Reading Standards for Literature
1. Refer to details and examples in a text when explaining what the text says explicitly and when drawing inferences from a text.
4. Determine the theme of a story, drama, or poem from details in a text; summarize the text.

Speaking and Listening Standards, grades K–5
1. Engage effectively in a range of collaborative discussions (one-on-one, in groups, and teacher-led) with diverse partners on grade 4 topics and texts, building on others' ideas and expressing their own clearly.

How Katie enacts the practice	←— Teaching Practice —→	How Scott enacts the practice
→ Uses ABCD cards and the Popsicle activity as a formative assessment to check understanding of theme. → Uses think-alouds to model her process for understanding theme in the texts. → Uses guided and independent reading to allow students to have the opportunity to practice discovering theme in texts.	Open a space for students to participate in a range of conversations and collaborations, while providing ongoing oral and written formative feedback to help students develop ideas and construct learning.	→ Uses student blog entries as formative assessment to ascertain students' understanding of theme. → Uses think-alouds to model his process for understanding theme in the texts. → Encourages pop-up debates in which students discuss and reflect on speeches. → Uses student conversations, both virtual and in-class, to guide instruction.
How Katie's students enact the practice	←— Learning Practice —→	**How Scott's students enact the practice**
→ Those who quickly grasp the concept of theme construct extended paragraphs using support from the text. → Write weekly, responding to what they have learned in the mini-lesson and what they have read independently. → Reflect on their understanding as a reader through an "exit slip."	Interact and share ideas with a partner, with a small group, with the whole class, and with the instructor. Respond to others' ideas and build understandings that take these into account.	→ Sit next to a preselected partner for quick activities such as Think-Pair-Share. → Meet together in a virtual small group through discussions on the class blog, where they can comment and discuss anonymously. → Use sticky notes in their books to record their thinking about the texts they read.

NCTE Principles
To foster active listening, teachers can encourage students to build upon one another's contributions to discussions.
Teachers must have routines for systematic assessment to ensure that each student is benefiting optimally from instruction.

See Appendix B for more on NCTE principles regarding instruction in reading and in speaking and listening. You can access the CCSS at http://www.corestandards.org/assets/CCSSI_ELA%20Standards.pdf.

Common Core State Standards That This Practice Supports

Reading Standards for Literature
1. Refer to details and examples in a text when explaining what the text says explicitly and when drawing inferences from a text.

Reading Standards: Foundational Skills
4. Read with sufficient accuracy and fluency to support comprehension.

Speaking and Listening Standards, grades K–5
1. Engage effectively in a range of collaborative discussions (one-on-one, in groups, and teacher-led) with diverse partners on grade 4 topics and texts, building on others' ideas and expressing their own clearly.

How Katie enacts the practice	←———— Teaching Practice ————→	How Scott enacts the practice
→ Uses small reading groups of four to six students organized based on information in Katie's formative assessment. → Uses a student to model finding textual support during reading. → Uses an extended writing activity to help more-advanced students synthesize concepts from the mini-lesson and the text itself.	Provides students with a variety of reading opportunities that allow a range of reading skills to be developed by each student.	→ Uses a gradual release of responsibility to shift students to independent reading. → Uses "mentor texts" to demonstrate to students a wide range of examples of theme. → Uses the class blog as a way for students to read one another's writing and practice responding as readers.
How Katie's students enact the practice	←———— Learning Practice ————→	**How Scott's students enact the practice**
→ Students answer multiple-choice questions about the reading in the whole-class group. → Students explain their answers to both multiple-choice and open-ended questions using selections of text from their reading. → Talk to other students in reading groups about their understanding of the text.	Talk to others—both their teacher and their classmates—about what they are reading. Practice strategies that allow them to approach texts that range from simple to difficult.	→ Use a prearranged pairing to efficiently discuss whole-class readings. → Use anonymous features of their class blog to interact with their fellow students' comments about the text. → Use strategies such as think-alouds and sticky-note markers to transition from group readings to independent readings.

NCTE Principles
Writing instruction must accommodate the explosion in technology from the world around us. Teachers should teach before-, during-, and after-reading strategies for constructing meaning of written language, including demonstrations and think-alouds.

See Appendix B for more on NCTE principles regarding instruction in reading and in speaking and listening. You can access the CCSS at http://www.corestandards.org/assets/CCSSI_ELA%20Standards.pdf.

Frames That Build: Exercises to Interpret the CCSS

The following are some exercises that may help you to individually or as a team work to interpret the CCSS in a way that makes sense for your teaching context.

- *Reading the standards.* With a group of teachers or on your own, look at the language of the reading standards and find specific places where students are expected to examine, explain, or analyze the themes of a text. Examine how the expectations change as students move up grade levels, and compare your analysis to your current curriculum. In what ways might you challenge your students to analyze and articulate the themes in a story?

- *Adapting practices for your context.* Consider ways in which you might adapt one or more of the practices employed by Katie or Scott for your classroom and students. Which practices or activities do you think will resonate with your students? Which practices fit particularly well into your interpretations of the CCSS and your already-established learning objectives? Which practices address areas of the CCSS that your current curriculum does not?

Getting to the Point: Determining Main Ideas and Summarizing Text

As a teenager, I began to understand that whenever I was talking to my grandmother, I was going to have to do some thinking to be able to understand her message. It wasn't that she spoke in metaphors or used difficult language; it was simply that her "train of thought" had no conductor—her tangents and inclusion of details unrelated to her points often left me wondering just where the conversation was headed or where we started from in the first place. As elementary teachers, if you've ever had to endure a student's recounting of an incident on the playground or accidentally asked a student to tell what he or she did over the weekend, you know that many elementary and intermediate students provide summaries that are chock full of details, tidbits, and wanderings that are not necessarily summaries. In my experience, teaching this critical communication skill is easier said than done and requires modeling and tremendous amounts of guided practice with feedback across many settings and text types to become second nature. The following vignettes show two teachers as they create the instructional settings necessary for this deep learning to happen.

Meet Jalynn Clayton,
Double Eagle Elementary School

Jalynn Clayton is a reflective practitioner who works within a diverse, urban setting in Albuquerque, New Mexico. She teaches fifth grade at Double Eagle Elementary School, which is one of the 89 elementary schools within the Albuquerque Public Schools (APS). Jalynn is a seasoned teacher and has taught fifth grade in this school for ten years. Albuquerque Public Schools serves 90,000 students, which is nearly a third of all the students in New Mexico. Like most urban districts, Albuquerque represents many distinct populations: 68 percent of students represent racial/ethnic diversity (Hispanic, African American, Native

American, and Asian/Pacific Islander), 17 percent are English language learners, with 15 percent of the students qualifying for special education services. Most challenging, however, is the fact that more than half of the students in the district are eligible for free or reduced-price lunch.

Jalynn is committed to excellence and to making a difference for her students. She creates routines and structures that foster learning and increase confidence for her students. Jalynn plans lessons that provide critical understandings about complex matters and then works with individuals and small groups to support these understandings in different ways to ensure that everyone has access to the curriculum and to her goals. Because of this, her students know that she cares and are thankful to learn in such a supportive environment.

Nonfiction Matters: Jalynn's Classroom

Common Core State Standards
The CCSS acknowledge the need for students to engage with and understand the structures of informational texts as well as fictional texts. Magazines such as *Sports Illustrated for Kids*, *Cricket*, *American Girl*, *Cobblestone*, or *Discovery Kids* are other excellent resources of quality informational texts appropriate for intermediate grade students.

Jalynn knows that teaching her students to identify main ideas and supporting details is not something that is accomplished in just one lesson but that it is taught and practiced on a continual basis that changes over time. At the start of the school year, Jalynn uses class periodicals such as *National Geographic for Kids* or *Scholastic News*. She reads the article aloud while her students follow along and explains that from time to time, she will stop to "think aloud" about what she thinks are the author's main ideas—the most important points the author is trying to make. Jalynn models in this way to make clear to her students the main ideas of the text, but this is not her only motivation for modeling. By modeling and sharing her thought process, she shows students *how* she came to know that something is a main idea. Toward the end of the article, she begins to involve students more in determining main ideas and uses questions to guide them toward supporting their thinking.

Another way that Jalynn teaches summarization early in the school year is through the use of the students' social studies textbooks. Though not a huge fan of textbooks, she does think it is important for children to know how to use these resources; in fact, Jalynn probably teaches them as much about reading as about particular social studies concepts when working in their textbooks. Jalynn also makes the students aware of particular text features—subtitles, headings, and sidebars—that often signal to the reader that a new main idea is present. For example, when reading about the American Revolution, she demonstrates that each section has a heading and each heading is about one particular aspect that is related to the topic—each one generally has a main idea and then a series of facts—details that support or elaborate on the main idea. As the year progresses or as a particular piece of text warrants, Jalynn finds new reasons to revisit the concept. Sometimes, informational texts that

Integrated Teaching and Learning

When teaching textual features like those Jalynn emphasizes here, teachers might consider using graphic organizers to help their students keep track of main ideas and details in an organized way that might later lead to a written or spoken summary of a section of text.

Honoring Diversity

Textual annotation can help students note thoughts without needing to interrupt their reading too obtrusively; if teachers' settings don't allow them to make copies, as Jalynn does here, teachers could supply students with sticky notes or color-coded sticky flags so that they can come back to the passage later.

Common Core State Standards

Even though the standards are broken up into different literate categories such as "reading," "writing," "language," and "listening and speaking," Jalynn recognizes the need to connect what students read to what they write. For more information on combining multiple standards within a single lesson or practice, see Section III of this volume or the charts at the end of each chapter.

students are exposed to have headings that are clever or involve plays on words that don't directly show the main idea. Teaching students how to identify patterns in the kinds of information found in a section leads them toward being able to infer the main ideas.

Throughout the year, regardless of the texts used, Jalynn uses Think/Pair/Share partners and small groups to provide scaffolded experiences with the concepts of main idea and supporting details. She sometimes gives the groups guiding questions that may lead them to think about the main ideas/supporting details and asks them to summarize their section in writing. She often provides students with photocopies of the article or textbook, asking them to independently mark up the text by highlighting or underlining main ideas and their supporting details. Jalynn uses all of these opportunities—small groups or independent applications—to formatively assess whether or not they understand the concept. She floats around the room, spot-checking—looking over shoulders, asking questions, and looking at their products to see whether students are successful. If she sees common mistakes across many students, Jalynn knows she needs to do more careful teaching within the large group. But, if most are getting it, she will instead meet with those who struggle with this concept individually or in a small-group setting to clear up confusion and reteach as needed. One particular problem that Jalynn is always watchful of is when some children pick red herrings as a main idea—they seem to be distracted by a detail that is interesting but not important. Jalynn thinks this is hard for many kids to grasp because, depending on their background knowledge, almost everything in an article is new information to the student and so it all seems important. With these cases, Jalynn knows that she must go further to show how authors use text features and repetition of the important ideas as a means of helping her students distinguish important from interesting information.

To achieve a greater depth of understanding, Jalynn reinforces this learning across many parts of her curriculum, giving students more meaningful contexts to see and use the concept. One such context is in her teaching of writing. By spring, she expects that her students are able to use summarization to help with organizing their own writing. Jalynn demonstrates how authors explain their topic in more detail by breaking the topic into several main ideas—big, important understandings that the reader should remember. She demonstrates to her students how if she were writing an informational report about sea urchins, her first section might be about their habitat, and then she lists the facts—the supporting details—about that aspect in that section. She continues showing how the next section might be about the food the urchins eat and how her last section might be about the life cycle of sea urchins. Making this important parallel to writing provides students the opportunity to see, from the inside, how authors break topics down into main ideas and how they support these main ideas by telling facts or details. Up to this point, Jalynn has had students focusing on reading and on identifying main ideas and details. She feels that when she brings these concepts into writing instruction, it "clicks" for them. Jalynn knows that it is the combination of all of these rich experiences over time that help kids sort out this difficult concept so that they are successful in their reading and writing lives.

Jalynn's Journey: Pathways to Enact These Practices

Early in Jalynn's teaching career, she was influenced greatly by another teacher who she refers to as "Book Whisperer." She was drawn to this colleague for many reasons: she had deep knowledge about how reading and writing worked, she had expertise with a variety of children's literature, and she displayed passion for teaching. In Jalynn's words, "I wanted to be her when I grew up!" This collegial relationship taught Jalynn the important lesson that teachers cannot wait passively for their district to provide the professional development they need. Under the wing of this colleague, Jalynn concluded that good reading and writing teachers have to read lots of professional books, written by people who actually teach kids how to read and write. She routinely read different articles in *The Reading Teacher* and more extensively from professional authors; Regie Routman, Katie Wood Ray, Carl Anderson, Ralph Fletcher, Donald Graves, and Lucy Calkins are among the many authors who influenced her teaching. To this day, Jalynn professes that she always has three or four professional books on her nightstand.

When asked how her approach to literacy teaching has changed over the span of her career, Jaylynn reflects that there have been major shifts. One change regards the pace of her literacy instruction—she doesn't push through things just to get through them. Instead, Jalynn is more concerned about doing fewer things but doing them better and going more in-depth. Because of her experiences reading professional books and her work with colleagues, Jalynn feels that she is a much better teacher of reading and writing than when she first started. She feels increasingly more relaxed and has come to trust herself more. Additionally, she feels that she does less for her students than in the past, encouraging them toward independence. Along with this, Jalynn feels that she now has higher expectation for students and works thoughtfully to make students more accountable for their learning.

Views on assessment have also changed for Jalynn over the years. Today, she reflects that she definitely uses a wider variety of assessments than when she first started teaching. She also now knows to develop and use a wider variety of ways for her students to be able to demonstrate their understanding. Jalynn believes that talking to and conferencing with students about the work they are doing and about the thinking they are engaged in provides valuable information that paper-and-pencil tests cannot provide. Using formative assessment has also become more prominent in Jalynn's classroom work. She previously relied heavily on larger assessments—big end-of-unit tests—to assess student learning. Now, she relies more on smaller, frequent formative assessments that happen throughout the learning process to guide her understanding of student progress and thus her future teaching decisions. She also tries to create performance assessments that meet the needs of different learning styles and to make assessment more interesting for students.

By far, the most important reflection of Jalynn's journey regards her understanding of her own learning path. In retrospect, she has come to understand that one doesn't become a great teacher of literacy by using someone else's program or from just doing what one professional resource says to do: "You have to take bits and pieces from each one. And, the same thing that I try to instill in my students is true for me as well: you have to be responsible for your own learning."

Meet Dana O'Brien, Baker Demonstration School

Dana O'Brien teaches third grade at Baker Demonstration School in Wilmette, Illinois, just north of Chicago. Baker is a private elementary school that caters to students in preK through eighth grades, and it has faced challenges in recent years as state and national standards movements have placed pressure on private elementary and middle schools whose students move on to public high schools. Dana has been a teacher for fourteen years and has taught at Baker for the last three years.

Dana has been teaching her current third-grade class for two years and will get a new second-grade class next year. When asked about her classroom demographics, Dana refers to many of the students individually, noting the unique characteristics, challenges, and strengths of each student in her class. She notes that one student is undergoing evaluation for ADD/ADHD, another suffers from anxiety, and a few struggle with reading at their grade level. She also notes individual students' particular strengths and uses those to encourage and enhance student learning, as evidenced in the story of one of her students, Jordan, in the following vignette.

Dana's classroom is all about student choice. Dana values the students' interests and sees to it that they follow up on their questions in meaningful ways that support literacy learning across subject areas. She knows each of her students as individuals and finds ways to challenge each of them in ways that will help them grow while still helping them feel comfortable and capable in the classroom. This snapshot follows Dana and her students as they learn about Greek mythology to create their own texts.

Exploring Summary through Journey Narratives: Dana's Classroom

Dana's school affords her a lot of freedom in her curricular planning, and the way in which she approaches concepts such as summarization is evidence of this. Dana is flexible in her planning and allows her students to shape how the class moves forward, what topics they cover, and what projects they develop; Dana uses a student-centered approach to facilitate students' learning around their needs and interests and addresses concepts such as summarization, inference, and theme throughout the year. Because of the curricular freedom Dana enjoys, she is able to decide what books she wants to use with her students, and she gives her students agency to make decisions with her. For example, before the end of the school year last year, Dana's second-grade students asked if they could read *The Lightning Thief*, a book from the popular Percy Jackson and the Olympians series. Dana knew that this would be a challenging book for such young students, so she chose to use it as a read-aloud book, to engage the students with supplementary texts on Greek mythology at their reading levels to support their class readings and discussions of the popular novel, and to integrate the unit into other parts of her curriculum.

Dana's goals for the unit included facilitating student learning about Greek mythology, exposing students to "journey narratives" and their characteristics, helping students summarize informative and narrative texts, and examining how heroes are constructed in narratives and how these stories and heroes relate to students' lives. Students engaged in oral and written summarization throughout the unit as they explored different Greek myths and compared them to *The Lightning Thief*, to other stories with heroic characters, and to their own experiences. Dana asked students to apply their learning to other aspects of her curriculum, as well. They discussed seeds and growth in science and imagined what Hades's mythological pomegranate farm must have looked like. They created a mural to depict the pomegranate farm using inspiration from modern art representing agriculture, and they used their studies of perimeter and area in mathematics to measure how much space they would have for their mural, which required students to integrate their literacy learning experiences

A student in Dana's classroom explains the class's mural of the Underworld.

into other subject areas—a practice strongly supported by the CCSS. The pictures here illustrate the students' work on their mural, which integrated art, science, mathematics, and English language arts in Dana's curriculum.

A typical day in Dana's classroom begins with literacy activities: students enter the classroom and read to themselves or finish a writing activity from the previous day. Then, the whole class comes together for a class meeting, during which the class discusses their day and reads a picture book or another

Students in Dana's classroom working together on the Underworld mural.

book related to their studies at the moment, such as *The Lightning Thief*. From there, students move into project work—if they are currently working on a project related to reading—or into book groups, which center around Gail Boushey and Joan Moser's (2006) "Daily Five": Read to Self, Read to Someone, Listen to Reading, Work on Writing, and Word Work. Students in Dana's classroom rotate in their groups to complete different tasks each morning, but Dana acknowledges the need to be flexible with these rotations, since they rarely have time to get through every rotation in a single day.

On one particular morning, a few of Dana's students are looking through *D'Aulaires' Book of Greek Myths* by Ingri and Edgar D'Aulaire, which contains illustrated stories of the major Greek gods and goddesses. They are reading it aloud to one another and connecting their reading to what they have learned from their *Lightning Thief* readings as a whole class. Puzzled by a story about Athena, they turn to *Oh My Gods!: A Look-It-Up Guide to the Gods of Mythology* by Megan E. Bryant, which clarifies their questions. Later, they will need to summarize their reading and to find the main idea of one of the Greek myths, which will require them to synthesize what they have learned from the two texts. Dana first supports this by asking students to tell her what they think the main idea of *Lightning Thief* might be. She lists the students' ideas on the board and then asks questions to help them narrow their focus, recording their thought processes as they come closer and closer to the main idea. She

Connections

Dana's students focus their studies on a single text—*The Lightning Thief*—but this is a fulcrum text, around which Dana places supplementary readings and other stories about Greek mythology. These supplemental texts make the more difficult Percy Jackson book easier to understand, and this also allows Dana to work with many types of texts—informational, dramatic, and fictional—within a single unit. For more information on using fulcrum texts in your instruction, see Section III.

then asks students to list the major events from the myth that led them to the main idea—this results in a class-composed summary that the students can use as a model for their own summaries of Greek myths later.

As students become more familiar with the concept of summarization, Dana begins teaching them what she calls the "five finger approach" to summarization. This approach associates a particular element of a story with one of the digits (or the palm) on the students' hands; thumb = characters, pointer finger = setting, middle finger = problem, ring finger = events, pinky finger = solution, and the palm = author's purpose or message—the main idea. Students write each "finger" for a story on an index card and use the index cards to create a summary, which helps them to understand which ideas to look for in a story and how to use those concepts to construct a summary and find a theme or main idea. To guide students toward being more independent, Dana starts by asking students to summarize parts of read-aloud texts like *The Lightning Thief*; once students illustrate comfort with summarization, they move on to summarize their independent reading texts. After the process is firmly set and easily recalled, the students move on to the index card method. Dana says, "This would occur after a read-aloud so that when we review it, it's easier to understand each other's answers. Eventually, the students become quite comfortable with the index cards and can from there write a paragraph summary without even thinking of the steps."

Honoring Diversity
Dana "breaks down" the task of writing a summary by helping students see the different parts of a summary. Other ways to do this might include using graphic organizers or modeling the process of writing a summary with the whole class before students write individually.

The students in Dana's classroom not only *write* summaries, though, they also use drama to act out their summaries. Dana's love of drama led her to incorporate this response to literature into her teaching and, with the help of her students, who assigned and imagined characters, they created a play about Greek mythology. Dana used her knowledge of each student's unique qualities to help them develop and perform their play; she writes of one student, "Jordan is a quiet kid, but when he gets on stage, he really comes to life. He is the type of kid that you can give a solo, tell him to make it bigger than life, and he hits the mark. So we made his character really big." Dana's instruction of the mythology unit illustrates her ability to appeal to different learning styles, draw on students' strengths to help them learn, and create an environment in which students can create and interact with texts from multiple genres, such as drama, narrative, and historical texts.

Honoring Diversity
Dana lets the needs and individual talents of her students dictate what will happen next in the curriculum—evidence of a curriculum that is truly student-centered.

Dana's Journey: Pathways to Enact These Practices

Dana's journey as an educator began with her parents and her own school experiences. When she was a middle school student, her drama teacher played a strong role in her development, helping Dana discover a love of theater that extended into her high school, college, and adult years. To this day, Dana performs improvisational comedy on stage weekly, which she has done since 1991. Her love of drama has affected her teaching by encouraging her to "think outside the box" when it comes to class projects and modes of expression. When asked about the impact of her love of drama on her teaching, Dana says, "Improv plays a huge part in how I do things in the classroom and in life." Dana has used her passion for the performing arts to shape her teaching, exciting the same thrill in her students during their mythology play and unit.

When asked about her first years of teaching, Dana says she felt lost, scared, and unsure about how to be a good teacher. While she notes that her education at the University of Chicago still leads her in her teaching, she acknowledges that she has learned a lot about herself as a teacher through becoming a parent and through learning from her colleagues and from her students. She explains that becoming a parent helped her to "see things from both perspectives," which has enabled her to better respond to her students' needs. Experience both as a mother and as a teacher taught Dana that she needs to not only listen to students but also respond in affirming and empowering ways to their ideas and reactions to texts and lessons. Over time, these transformations in how she approaches her relationships with students have led her to adopt a more student-centered approach to planning. When asked about her approach to teaching the mythology unit the way she did, Dana says:

> This is kind of how I do things. We do have specific units of study, but within the units, there is much flexibility. So, I like to give the basics to the kids and then see where they take it. It keeps it different every year and makes it relevant to the class I have. They feel ownership over the studies and therefore are more invested in the outcomes.

Connections

For planning resources to help you think about integrating the CCSS into a student-centered classroom, see the examples and resources in Section III.

Dana's position as the team leader of the first through fifth grades gives her opportunities to discuss lesson plans with colleagues, collaborate on units across disciplines, and learn more about her students' needs and interests. Dana notes the importance of talking to her colleagues as she is planning units and lessons; she says that "talking things through with people" inspires her to try new things in the classroom. Dana also points out the importance of watching other teachers teach—she and her colleagues observe one another's instruction to help them reflect on and reinvent their own practices.

Charting the Practices

Both of these vignettes illustrate how lessons that work well include an integration of multiple literacy strands—reading, writing, speaking, listening, and language.

Specifically, however, our two vignettes function as powerful examples of the importance of helping students develop reading and writing skills alongside one another. The charts below show how these teachers address specific standards in the CCSS in concert with NCTE principles to shape their teaching practices. The charts also include the learning practices students are expected to exhibit in response to the teaching practices.

Common Core State Standards That This Practice Supports

Reading Standards for Literature, grade 5
2. Determine the theme of a story, drama, or poem from details in the text, including how characters in a story or drama respond to challenges or how the speaker in a poem reflects upon a topic; summarize the text.

Writing Standards, grade 5
3. Write narratives to develop real or imagined experiences or events using effective technique, descriptive details, and clear event sequences.

Reading Standards for Informational Texts, grade 5
2. Determine two or more main ideas of a text and explain how they are supported by key details; summarize the text.

How Jalynn enacts the practice	◄──── Teaching Practice ────►	How Dana enacts the practice
→ Shows students how texts scaffold themselves through an analysis of genre in informational texts, like their content-area textbooks. → Scaffolds the tasks of breaking down main idea and supporting details by having students first work in pairs, then in small groups.	Uses a paralleled reading and writing approach to scaffold learning by breaking complex concepts into smaller, meaningful parts that connect and build toward greater understanding.	→ Uses the "five finger" method to break summaries into their multiple parts. → Records student thoughts about the important events in the story and helps them find the main idea. → Uses the "Daily Five" to engage students in writing and reading activities that complement one another.
How Jalynn's students enact the practice	◄──── Learning Practice ────►	**How Dana's students enact the practice**
→ Record their thinking in graphic organizers and annotate their texts as they read. → Use guiding questions to support their progress as they read. → Refine and complicate their own ideas and interpretations.	Students take responsibility for their own learning, which enables them to independently identify main idea and support their own thinking.	→ Shape instructional decisions by sharing their interests with the teacher and choosing what they read. → Use reading knowledge to write journey narratives.

NCTE Principles
Teachers should try to use a variety of instructional groupings, including whole group, small group, and individual instruction, to provide multiple learning experiences.

See Appendix B for more on NCTE principles regarding instruction in reading and writing. You can access the CCSS at http://www.corestandards.org/assets/CCSSI_ELA%20Standards.pdf.

Common Core State Standards That This Practice Supports

Reading Standards for Literature, grade 5
2. Determine the theme of a story, drama, or poem from details in the text, including how characters in a story or drama respond to challenges or how the speaker in a poem reflects upon a topic; summarize the text.

Speaking and Listening, grade 5
2. Summarize a written text read aloud or information presented in diverse media and formats, including visually, quantitatively, and orally.

Writing Standards, grade 5
3. Write narratives to develop real or imagined experiences or events using effective technique, descriptive details, and clear event sequences.

How Jalynn enacts the practice	◄—— Teaching Practice ——►	How Dana enacts the practice
→ Demonstrates think-alouds of the author's main idea to students as she reads class periodicals. → Questions students to guide them toward independent discovery of main idea. She also uses questions as a way of helping students as they learn to support their own thinking. → Discusses textbook genre features with students and helps them practice using the conventions of a textbook to discover main idea in informational texts.	Uses a "spiraling" approach to plan curriculum that demonstrates summarization to students in multiple ways throughout the school year.	→ Uses read-aloud books as a way of approaching more difficult texts with students. → Uses a variety of sources on Greek myths with students to support their summarization of *The Lightning Thief*. → Has the whole class participate in composing a collaborative summarization, which will later aid them in writing their own myth. → Uses the "five finger" summarization technique to help students grow comfortable in summarizing independently read texts.
How Jalynn's students enact the practice	◄—— Learning Practice ——►	**How Dana's students enact the practice**
→ Practice using summary as an organizational tool in their own writing. → Use features of the textbook genre to hunt down main idea and avoid red herrings. → Learn to explain how they came to their answers through think-alouds.	Students use strategies to develop independent discovery of main idea and supporting details in a variety of texts.	→ Synthesize material from a variety of sources to summarize myths and then compose their own myths and dramas. → Use the five finger technique to help them summarize and organize the myths they write. → Use drama to creatively display their understanding of the main ideas of Greek myths.

NCTE Principles
Teaching is a professional endeavor, and teachers are active problem-solvers and decision-makers in the classroom.

See Appendix B for more on NCTE principles regarding reading and writing instruction and speaking and listening. You can access the CCSS at http://www.corestandards.org/assets/CCSSI_ELA%20Standards.pdf.

Frames That Build: Exercises to Interpret the CCSS

The following are a few exercises for individual or teams of teachers to use to work more with the standards and see how these vignettes may provide a lens through which to view your own interpretation and individualized implementation of the standards.

- *Reading the standards.* Read the writing, speaking/listening, and reading standards and look for places where students might be asked to summarize a text, provide a summary of their ideas, or find the main ideas within a text. Highlight all of these places and consider lessons that might speak across literacy strands to meet multiple standards and engage students in multiple literate practices.

- *Working across genres.* Students today need to be able to navigate multiple types of text, all of which have different demands on both their composers and their readers. Jalynn incorporates structural analysis of informational texts to help her students understand the "clues" that will lead them toward the main idea. Dana incorporates multiple genres into her study of Greek mythology. Write down all of the genres with which you engage your students and consider your approach to those genres. How can you raise students' textual awareness as both readers and writers as you move across genres and engage students with many types of text?

Inferring with Support:
The Heart of Comprehension

ll students come to us knowing how to infer in their daily lives—without literal language they can all tell you what you should wear if you see it raining outside, how their mother might be feeling when she uses their full name, and what their best friend is feeling when faced with the death of a pet. This ability to infer comes naturally to humans and yet is often considered to be one of the deficit areas for intermediate students. Why is this? Many times, there seems to be a deficit because we have not attempted to build on student strengths and because we confuse making an inference and supporting it in writing as one and the same. The assumption that intermediate students should be able to convey their thinking in writing is not helpful because the vast majority have never been taught how to support their thinking. Here oral language is our first and best friend on the journey toward inferring.

Meet Erin Meyer, Countryside Elementary

Erin Meyer is an energetic and dynamic young teacher who works in Olathe, Kansas, a large suburb of Kansas City with approximately 27,000 students. For the first three years of her teaching career, Erin has taught fifth grade at Countryside Elementary, one of Olathe's elementary buildings. Countryside Elementary rivals many urban districts in its make-up with 29 percent English language learners, 28 percent African American, and 56 percent of students who qualify for free and reduced-price lunch. In the larger Olathe district as a whole, the demographics are different and include 26.4 percent racial diversity, 7.4 percent English language learners, 11.6 percent special education, and 23 percent economically disadvantaged students. As is evident in Erin's setting, across such a large district, individual school profiles can vary drastically. Erin's classroom at Countryside Elementary is even more diverse than the overall district, in which 50 percent of her students are classified as ELL.

Because of this linguistic and cultural diversity as well as many other factors, Erin and her teammates have moved toward using forms of differentiated instruction to ensure that they are meeting the specific needs present within their grade level. Erin understands the importance of cultural and linguistic differences and works sensitively to capitalize on these differences. She knows that high expectations and high-quality instruction will allow her to teach so that students achieve, using differentiation to meet the specific needs of all her students. Simply being aware of these factors is one thing, but putting them into action is quite another. Erin works diligently and collaboratively to make this happen every day.

Connections

Even though the CCSS do not set guidelines for students with diverse linguistic backgrounds, teachers need to find ways to teach students with many and varied language experiences. For more information on the CCSS and ELL students, see Section I.

Start with What They Know: Erin's Classroom

One of the most important strategies that Erin wants her students to grasp well is how to make and support an inference. Because Erin knows that this strategy develops over time, is honed and tuned according to the demands of increasingly difficult texts, and is ever-present in the lives of all readers, she plans not for isolated instruction at one point in the year, but rather focuses her students on the concept from the first days of school onward. Early in the school year, Erin is deliberate in her language and teaching to set the stages for inferring. Beginning with classroom management—in her room the set of student and teacher agreed-on rules are called "class agreements"—Erin builds the foundations of inferring by using real-life situations. She begins by listing things that the students can count on from her as the teacher, explaining to her students that if they think something in the classroom or school is unfair, they have the right to discuss that with her privately. She further explains that making a case for or against something requires thought and the collection of evidence or reasons to support an argument. She empowers the students to have a voice in the decision making of the classroom as much as possible, but emphasizes the need for supporting thinking with reasons—a deliberate move on her part to parallel what she will simultaneously emphasize in their reading conversations.

Common Core State Standards

Here, Erin uses the students' everyday lives to teach a concept such as inference. Teachers could use students' everyday lives to explore inferences in other ways that address multiple standards, too; for example, students could write short stories about their families or friends and their classmates could infer character traits from those stories.

After setting this important stage, Erin also engages the students in some specific language about inferring, using the class agreements as a model text. She gives her students a scenario of watching a group of children on the playground who are whispering and pointing at another student and then laughing and running away. Given this evidence, she asks her students to draw conclusions about what she, as the teacher, might be thinking is happening. The students correctly identify that there may be some unfriendly behaviors at play that would violate some of their agreements to treat others with respect. Erin also explains that just seeing only part of those same behaviors, such as gathering and whispering, would not be enough evidence to support a conclusion like this—for conclusions to be valid, she asserts that readers must have multiple layers of evidence. Using these concrete examples, she scaffolds her students' understanding of the more abstract concept of inferring and supporting their thinking.

Common Core State Standards

Here, Erin uses informational texts to teach inference instead of using literary texts, which also contain a lot of inference. Teachers might also consider how to approach inference with literary texts and discuss with students the differences between finding inferences in literary texts and finding them in informational texts. This approach could increase students' metacognitive engagement with inference.

Throughout the year and across the content areas, Erin is deliberate about using terms such as *inferring, drawing conclusions,* and *creating hypotheses,* always with an eye toward using evidence to support such thinking. During her reading block, described as a reading workshop with students working daily in flexible groups, Erin continually calls for inferential thinking and support throughout every reading experience. Erin uses graphic organizers not merely to test how well they have read something but also as a means of remembering important information and for seeing relationships between information; rather than having students simply fill in a story map to check comprehension, Erin knows that students need deeper experiences. For example, one group of students working within an informational article is asked to code their reading with an A for things that tell what the passage is about and an R for things that remind them of something else. Then, students transfer this thinking onto the "Reminds and About" graphic organizer. Here, several important things are at play: students are determining importance as they read, coding places where there is important information about the content of the article, and simultaneously engaging metacognitively, noticing what connections to prior knowledge they are making and what new understandings or questions they are bringing to the text, which often involves opportunities for inferring. When the group shares its individual thinking, Erin guides the students to deeper understandings about the text and about the importance of how background knowledge helps with inferring.

In another flexible group, this time working in the nonfiction text *Freedom Train,* by Dorothy Sterling, Erin continues to challenge her students' inferences with more complex questions. After reading one section of the text, Erin asks the students, "What analogy can be made from what you know from this section to what was happening in the larger setting of the country at this time?" Though her students struggle at first, her scaffolding of the vocabulary of the question soon opens a new and deeper understanding of what the text is telling us—the more elaborate inferences that can be drawn from taking the literal information into another, larger context. In both situations, Erin is able to employ reflective/responsive teaching to take students from where they are to new and deeper understandings about the text, about inferring, and about themselves as readers.

Despite this deliberate and ongoing language about inference during the year, some students continue to struggle with this and other concepts at the fifth-grade level. Erin and her team have come up with another structure for addressing student needs. Using data from both classroom experiences and from past assessments, the team identifies students who have exhibited difficulty with a particular concept. During the first thirty minutes of the day, children are divided into groupings that cross homerooms—some of Erin's students will go to work with her other colleagues and some of their children will come to her room. During this time, a weekly focus—inferring, summarizing, identifying main ideas, etc.—is established by the teachers. Using cooperative learning groups, the teachers use various creative and different ways to reteach the concepts to strengthen understandings through experiences. For example, for inferring, cooperative groups may use drama or charades to act out a situation or character, while others infer what is happening or what the character is feeling. These experiences and language-rich collaborative groups increase students' access to multiple perspectives and different teaching styles. Because students are helping one another in new and meaningful ways, motivation and engagement are high. All students, particularly ELL students and students with special needs, benefit from the increased use of language during this time, and student achievement data illustrate that this approach has helped. Since implementing these extra times, 85.8 percent of students from low-income families have passed state assessments in reading and 81.2 percent of ELL students have been successful as well!

Collaboration

Collaboration with colleagues enables Erin to be "on the same page" with her fellow teachers. By planning and setting instructional goals together, they are able to focus their instruction on specific objectives.

Erin's Journey: Pathways to Enact These Practices

Erin has taught only fifth grade in the Olathe district and has been teaching for three years. As an early-career teacher, Erin reflects that her undergraduate program at Emporia State University (ESU) was exemplary in preparing her for the rigors of being a successful teacher. According to Erin, Emporia State has a program with Olathe in which student teachers transition into being a teacher through a full-year internship. During this time, interns must attend not only the ESU core classes but also all classroom professional development that Olathe provides to teachers. This allows interns the opportunity to receive exemplary professional development in addition to having a chance to try out the strategies presented to interns. Erin attributes her successful transition into the profession partly to this experience.

Erin's district employs many district-level, on-site professional development opportunities, as well as providing access to outside resources. The district reading specialist offers consistent and ongoing training for teachers, showcasing new research and best practices for immediate and easy implementation into the

Connections

For more professional development tools and questions to guide individual teacher reflection, see Section III.

classroom. One such inservice that influenced Erin focused on the use of graphic organizers, where she learned about the "RAN" graphic organizer (see Figure 4.1). Erin quickly realized how immensely beneficial it could be and now uses it extensively in her reading and science lessons.

Erin's principal is also a collaborative force, offering support at the building level—helping Erin set goals, observing her teach, and offering quality feedback. Another influence on Erin has been the collaboration she engages in within her fifth-grade team. Erin has a special bond with one teammate who attended the same university as Erin, and now they are both working on their graduate degrees together. Erin reports that it is easier to make great instruction accessible when there are multiple team members all moving in the same direction, doing what is best for all students because they share the same philosophy and research-based approach. She clarifies that this is not about a scripted program, where everyone says the same things each day; instruction certainly looks different in each person's room and group, but everyone is working with the same goals in mind.

All of these factors—district-level, building-level, and team-level support—have had a positive impact on Erin's early career. Erin says, "we are 'customer focused' at our building and that means that our focus is on how we as a staff make sure our students are leaving us prepared for their future. Collaboration is the only way to make it work effectively and ensure that everyone is giving the best instruction they can."

Currently, Erin has been influenced by brain-based research books and classes and has become focused on converting information she has studied about how the brain learns into instruction that will ensure that she meets the individual needs of each student. Erin has taken several classes on brain-based learning, differentiation, and on questioning techniques. Another influence for Erin has been the work of Stephanie Harvey and Anne Goudvis in their book *Strategies That Work* (2007). This

RAN Chart				
What I think I know	Confirmed	Connections	New Learning	Wonderings
	Misconceptions			

FIGURE 4.1: RAN chart that Erin uses to help her reflect on her instruction.

resource offer helpful mini-lesson ideas for reading that are geared toward engaging students in meaningful literacy tasks and metacognitive thinking. Erin reflects that her effectiveness as a teacher has been enhanced with the different tools available to her through continuing education.

Erin is a lifelong learner by nature and is grateful for the experiences that continually shape her, and she reflects on her journey in this way: "I am a food lover, so the best way I can relate to this is by food. I like to believe that I was a quality grape, grown in an exceptional vineyard. I was then hand-picked with care and allowed to age in a proper environment to ensure that I would become a vintage wine of great value."

Meet Kelley Kyff, Salem Elementary

Kelley Kyff is a fifth-grade teacher at an elementary school in Michigan. Kelley began her teaching career seven years ago and has been teaching fifth grade for the past three years. Kelley's school is in a suburb of Oakland County, but it lies on the outskirts of the district. Most of the 314 students in the school are Caucasian, but the district's location gives the school diversity in terms of the socioeconomic status of its students. The school is rural, but the district lines also include more urban areas and a few neighborhoods of upper-middle-class homes. Kelley's school is classified as a Title I school and has a magnet program for gifted/talented students, which is housed in a separate building.

Kelley's general education classroom is an average size. Three of her students have been identified as emotionally impaired; two have learning disabilities in reading, writing, and math; and nearly a third of her students qualify for Title I. Kelley has support for these students through an inclusion model that places a Title I teacher in her classroom. Kelley describes her classroom as "a great mix of personalities," but she says that she works hard to maintain a positive classroom culture with her diverse group.

Much of Kelley's language arts instruction revolves around discussion and reading/writing workshops. Kelley says that she has worked hard to maintain a positive classroom culture, one where her students feel they can participate openly in discussion with each other. Kelley describes herself as being "protective" of the environment she has created and admits that she is careful to scaffold assignments and discussions so that her students, who have varying life experiences, can all participate fully.

Moving Inference into Writing: Kelley's Classroom

Before Kelley begins teaching a writing unit on the genre of personal essays, she introduces it by spending time explicitly teaching students about one aspect of inferring—how to infer writer purpose and genre characteristics. Kelley uses a fulcrum text to model for students how to "notice and name." That is, she demonstrates for them how to notice the elements of the genre and name what those elements are. It is important to Kelley that her students do not stop there, however. She also wants them to infer the author's purpose in using those characteristics and strategies so that they can later use those same strategies and characteristics in their own writing.

Integrated Teaching and Learning

Kelley's use of her own writing helps her students see her as a fellow learner and writer. Teachers also do this by modeling metacognitive processes in think-aloud activities, which help their students understand that knowledge is constructed and learned over time.

Kelley scaffolds this skill for her students in several ways. First, when she plans her curriculum for the year, she places a unit of nonfiction reading and writing directly before her writing unit on the personal essay. She says that this gives her students common ground for discussion and prompts writing topics for their personal essays. In fact, Kelley says that she incorporates informational texts throughout the year by using the students' social studies textbook to create reading lessons (along with a variety of other nonfiction texts). Many of her students do not have the life experiences to inform class discussions and essays, so these texts are crucial for "leveling the playing field" and giving all students an equal voice. In a previous unit on narrative writing, Kelley used a piece of her own writing as her mentor text and found that her students were excited to use their teacher's writing as a model. In this lesson, she has decided to utilize that earlier excitement by again using one of her own essays as a mentor text.

Kelley uses a readers workshop model of instruction, so she begins the lesson by reading the mentor text aloud for students. She instructs the students to watch as she reads "to notice." Kelley tells the students to read the text through once for comprehension and then models this step. Next, Kelley tells the students that she is going to read again for the purpose of noticing genre characteristics, stopping to model the "notice and name" technique and to explain why she, as an author, made these choices. Student agency is important to Kelley, so having her students explain author purpose supports her goal of having students understand the strategies that they (and other writers) use in different genres. While Kelley teaches inference explicitly at the beginning of the year using a T-chart, she finds that this explicit instruction is not enough to help students understand the inferences that they make naturally. Kelley finds that students can often make these inferences as they read a text, but they cannot support their conclusions about author purpose.

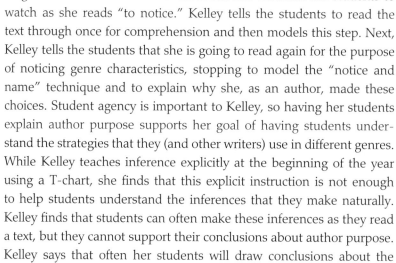

Connections

T-charts are graphic organizers that can help students keep track of the inferences they make when they read. Templates can be found online and in many graphic organizer resources for teachers. Other graphic organizers could also help students keep track of and visualize the inferences they make as they read.

Kelley says that often her students will draw conclusions about the author's purpose, and she points out to them, "You just made an inference!" Her students just need a way to support these conclusions, so teaching them to "notice and name" authorial strategies gives students a resource for supporting their inferences about a text. Kelley's goal for her students is for them to be able to make inferences about an author's strategies and purpose and support those inferences with the text through noticing and naming them.

To support this goal of student agency, Kelley has her students work in small groups. Her groupings are flexible, so they often change. She instructs the students to follow the steps she has modeled for them of reading the text through once for understanding, then reading it again to notice and name the characteristics of the personal essay and noting those things on the text. As the students work, Kelley confers with each group and addresses any problems they have. She reteaches the noticing and naming strategy for any groups that are having trouble. Throughout the rest of the unit on the personal essay, Kelley will use the workshop model to help students develop their writing. She says that usually, after her mini-lesson, students will read or write independently using their individual book bags. Her students also keep weekly reader-response journals, where they write about topics related to the genre they are reading and writing about in workshop or about their use of strategies. She often uses these journals as a formative assessment, as it clearly shows her when students are not "getting it." She responds in more detail to these students and uses their individual conference time to discuss their entries and address issues of confusion. Kelley uses this combination of guided independent learning and direct instruction to reach her goal of having students learn to infer about genre characteristics and author purpose—and more importantly, to explain how and why those characteristics and purposes work together within a text.

Honoring Diversity
Teachers can execute the "individual book bag" strategy using baskets for individual students or other organizational techniques. In schools where books are more communal, students might keep individualized lists of books that cater to their literacy needs.

Kelley's Journey: Pathways to Enact These Practices

Kelley's mother and grandmother are both teachers, and this early exposure to the "world of education" shaped her first years as a teacher. She says that many of the choices she made in her early career were because it "just felt right." Her classes' state standardized test scores were good in those early years, but she felt as though something was missing. Kelley says that the biggest change between those first couple of years and her teaching today is that she is now much more intentional in her instruction. Kelley spent a few years teaching fourth grade and then taught a schedule that included both fourth- and fifth-grade classes before moving to the fifth grade three years ago. Through this experience, she learned to think about curriculum as a whole, which is something that has strongly influenced what she emphasizes in her classroom. Kelley says that keeping a focus on developing her students as lifelong learners and thinking about what strategies they will need years down their educational road has made her think more about *why* these strategies are useful for students. As she says, "If they're just saying the right things, I used to be okay with that, but that's

not enough anymore. I want them to show me why they're making those choices. . . .
I want them to own those strategies."

When she first entered the profession, a focus of her teaching preparation was the
practice of guided reading and using a workshop model, but Kelley struggled with
the idea, feeling as if it wasn't enough for her students. However, Kelley quickly dis-
covered that individual conferencing, explicit instruction through mini-lessons, and
workshop experiences did help her meet her goal of giving her students
agency over their own learning. Kelley feels that this shift in her percep-
tions of what defines "good" teaching has greatly benefited her students.

Kelley's work with her district's math standards committee introduced
her to the Common Core State Standards, and she began using them
for planning shortly after this introduction. Her work with the Oakland
Writing Project also encouraged her to begin using the standards for planning purposes. Though she says she still uses the Michigan standards, as
those are currently the ones she is held accountable for, Kelley makes sure
that her lessons are beginning to cover the CCSS as well.

Connections

For more information on
the standards themselves,
see Section I; for information about planning and
integrating the standards
into your existing curriculum, see Section III.

Over the past few years, Kelley has also begun to plan a little differently than she
did in the beginning. The fourth- and fifth-grade teachers at her school have formed
an informal collaborative planning team, which meets weekly (and more often as
needed) to work together and to ensure that the grade-level curricula align vertically.
In addition to her collaborative planning, Kelley also participates in her school's math
standards committee and the Oakland Writing Project and says that these
collaborations shape her teaching in positive ways. Through these opportunities, Kelley has developed a reflective teaching practice that has obvi-
ously led her to be a thoughtful practitioner—adapting her teaching style
to give her students more agency and working on being a more intentional instructor. She has developed the habit of choosing one element of
her teaching every year and spends that year focusing on developing that
aspect of her teaching practice. Kelley says that this has helped her not be
overwhelmed, especially in the first few years of her career.

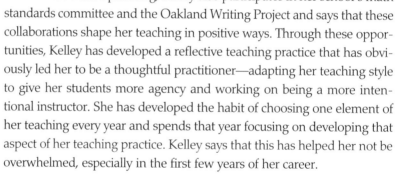

Collaboration

Kelley challenges herself
to try one new practice
each year; this could be a
fun challenge to engage in
with a close colleague or
as a team or department.
Consider ways you might
adopt or adapt Kelley's
challenge.

Charting the Practices

In both vignettes, teachers began with students' knowledge to move toward something bigger and deeper with inferring. The use of gradual release—the pattern of
modeling and demonstration followed by guided practice with feedback toward
increasing independence with less support over time—is evident in both classrooms.

Common Core State Standards That This Practice Supports

Reading Standards for Informational Texts, grade 5
1. Quote accurately from a text when explaining what the text says explicitly and when drawing inferences from the text.
8. Describe how reasons support specific points the author makes in a text.

Writing Standards, grade 5
9. Draw evidence from literary or informational texts to support analysis, reflection, and research.

Speaking and Listening Standards, grade 5
3. Engage effectively in a range of collaborative discussions (one-on-one, small group, and teacher-led) with diverse partners on grade 5 topics and texts, building on others' ideas and expressing their own clearly.

How Erin enacts the practice	◄──── Teaching Practice ────►	How Kelley enacts the practice
→ Finds graphic organizers to help students visualize their thoughts about abstract concepts. → Proposes real-life situations where students encounter problems and guides them to consider solutions to help them understand how to use evidence to support their thinking.	Use real-life situations as model texts, in order to demonstrate abstract concepts and enhance student understanding.	→ Uses her own writing as a mentor text, showing that she is a fellow writer and learner. → Uses informational texts as mentor texts to help students practice drawing conclusions and finding support for them using facts. → Models "noticing and naming" to demonstrate inference and encourage students' metacognition.
How Erin's students enact the practice	◄──── Learning Practice ────►	**How Kelley's students enact the practice**
→ Code elements of a text in a graphic organizer that helps them connect prior knowledge to their reading. → "Think like a teacher" when they are given a hypothetical playground situation using prior knowledge and observations to make inferences. → Use evidence gathered from a text to support their inferences in whole-group discussions.	Use metacognition to connect new ideas to prior knowledge and to recognize when they are making inferences.	→ "Notice and name" evidence from text to support inference. → Record "noticings" in journals to determine authorial purpose. → Listen and respond to teacher feedback. → Connect their prior knowledge of the characteristics of a narrative to their writing of a personal essay.

NCTE Principles
Teachers should know their students as individuals, including their interests, their attitudes about reading, and their school, home, and community experiences.
Teachers should gradually release instructional responsibility to support independent reading.

See Appendix B for more on NCTE principles regarding reading and writing instruction and speaking and listening. You can access the CCSS at http://www.corestandards.org/assets/CCSSI_ELA%20Standards.pdf.

Common Core State Standards That This Practice Supports

Reading Standards for Informational Texts, grade 5
1. Quote accurately from a text when explaining what the text says explicitly and when drawing inferences from the text.
8. Describe how reasons support specific points the author makes in a text.

Speaking and Listening, College and Career Readiness, grade 5
3. Identify the reasons and evidence a speaker provides to support particular points.

Writing Standards, grade 5
9. Draw evidence from literary or informational texts to support analysis, reflection, and research.

Speaking and Listening Standards, grade 5
3. Engage effectively in a range of collaborative discussions (one-on-one, small group, and teacher-led) with diverse partners on *grade 5 topics and texts*, building on others' ideas and expressing their own clearly.

How Erin enacts the practice	◄—— Teaching Practice ——►	How Kelley enacts the practice
→ Introduces the concept of inference through classroom contracts at the beginning of the year, showing students that inference is something they already do. → Consistently uses "inference vocabulary" so students are deliberate about their identification of inference in their daily reading. → Uses daily reading activities to create an opportunity for students to practice supporting inferences with evidence.	Scaffolds inference skills so students learn to support their thinking and assertions about texts.	→ Uses mentor texts to help students make inferences about authorial purpose. → Uses information from prior units to scaffold her unit on the personal essay, which gives all students common topics for writing. → Models inference through think-alouds so that students can learn to explain their thinking. → Gives students a pattern for their reading in collaborative groups, which allows them a comfortable structure to work from.
How Erin's students enact the practice	◄—— Learning Practice ——►	**How Kelley's students enact the practice**
→ Use graphic organizers to help themselves see connections among texts. → Adopt their teacher's vocabulary as a way of gaining a language to talk about a skill they have practiced outside the classroom. → Use cooperative learning activities to gain knowledge from other students.	Use organizational strategies and skills to develop inference.	→ Use their "noticings" and understanding of authorial purpose to make their own writing more purposeful. → Use journals to demonstrate their understanding of texts and show the support for their inferences. → Connect their prior knowledge through life experience and readings to their work as writers.

NCTE Principles
Teachers should teach before-, during-, and after-reading strategies for constructing meaning of written language, including demonstrations and think-alouds.
Teachers should gradually release instructional responsibility to support independent reading.

See Appendix B for more on NCTE principles regarding reading and writing instruction and speaking and listening. You can access the CCSS at http://www.corestandards.org/assets/CCSSI_ELA%20Standards.pdf.

Frames That Build: Exercises to Interpret the CCSS

The following are a few exercises for individual or teams of teachers to use to work more with the standards and see how these vignettes may provide a lens through which to view your own interpretation and individualized implementation of the standards.

- *Read the standards.* With colleagues or on your own, read the standards with an eye toward places where they ask students to engage in complex cognitive processes such as *inference.* As we mentioned in the introduction to this section, inferring is something we do every day as humans, but often students struggle to wrap their minds around these complex, and sometimes unconscious, tasks. Imagine ways you might metacognitively engage your students and share ideas with your colleagues.

- *Find resources that empower and enable you and your students.* Kelley and Erin approach inference in different ways with their students: Erin's students label their texts, while Kelley's use graphic organizers to help them keep track of their ideas. Both of these ideas, when paired with scaffolded instruction and modeling, help students engage in complex metacognitive thought processes. Consider what resources you use to teach inference and how these work (or do not work) for your students. What other resources exist in your school? What resources do other teachers use to teach inference?

Looking Backward to Move Forward

Katie, Scott, Jalynn, Dana, Erin, and Kelley are exemplary teachers, but they would be the first to say that they learn constantly from colleagues around them, and that they have moments of despair as well as moments of great joy as they face frustrations and challenges every day. They understand the importance of putting standards in perspective as resources as well as the importance of getting involved and taking action when they find that standards or other mandates are unjust or poorly grounded. They know that standards cannot replace the professional knowledge of a great teacher, a teacher's deep knowledge of the children in his or her classroom, or a teacher's commitment to contributing to the growth of human beings who have the skills and dispositions to make a difference in the world.

Before moving forward to considering how you might plan your own instruction, take time to think back to the vignettes and journeys offered by the teachers included in this section. Look across grade levels and demographics, taking care not to reject ideas when classrooms do not look and sound exactly like your own. The following discussion questions can help you look more closely at the vignettes and journeys.

Teaching and Learning Strategies

- Consider the specific teaching and learning strategies used by the teachers in this book. How are they similar and different?
- How do these teachers demonstrate knowledge of the strengths and needs of their students?
- What are some of the resources these teachers call on to foster learning?

Valuing and Using Students' Home Language(s) and Knowledge

- How do these teachers demonstrate that they value students from many different cultural and linguistic backgrounds?
- How do these teachers learn about and use students' families and communities as resources?
- How do these teachers use the resources that students bring to the classroom as foundational to their teaching?

Incorporating Formative Assessment into Instruction

- What strategies of formative assessment are demonstrated in these vignettes?
- How do teachers use formative assessment to keep track of student progress throughout a unit of study?

Recognizing the Power of Collaboration

- As you read through the vignettes and journeys of individual teachers, what instances of collaboration do you find?
- As the teacher journeys show, reflection on practice is a key part of professional growth. Take an instance of collaboration; how does it foster teacher reflection?

Incorporating Various Technologies into Instruction

- What technologies do these teachers use in their instruction?
- How do these uses of technology foster student learning?

Expanding the Teaching Repertoire

- Which of the teaching strategies demonstrated here might you use in your own classroom?
- How would you need to adapt this strategy to meet the learning needs of your students?

Aligning Teaching with Curricular Requirements and Standards

- What can you infer about how these teachers meet curricular requirements while still addressing students' learning needs?
- How would you describe the ways these teachers meet a rich array of the CCSS while focusing first on their students and their knowledge of good teaching?

The next section of this book suggests ways you can plan to integrate the CCSS into your own teaching and work with colleagues to develop more extensive programs of instruction.

III

Building

⊚ Introduction

At this point, you may be thinking to yourself, *Where do I begin?* There are many concerns competing for your attention as a teacher. Many students with diverse needs pass through your classroom door on a daily basis, and you have developed outcomes, goals, and objectives to guide your instruction in meeting these students' needs. And to this end, you have established practices and ways of assessing student learning in your classroom. You bring your professional pedagogical content knowledge to the classroom, providing expertise in reading, writing, speaking, and listening for students. You teach within a specific context as well, considering the needs of your community and the demographic populations that you serve. With so many issues pressing in on teachers from all directions, aligning and shifting your teaching practices with the CCSS may feel like one more task heaped onto your already full plate.

Getting started by pulling back to view the big picture may help to put things into perspective and make first steps seem less overwhelming. As Figure 5.2 (p. 71) suggests, considering the CCSS as part of the deliberate teaching and learning choices you already make can continue to help you keep students at the center of instruction while planning, enacting teaching practices, and assessing student learning.

Just as most of us could not wake up one morning and decide to run a marathon on will alone without significant prior conditioning, so too it is important to remind yourself that planning, teaching, and assessing with the CCSS will not be instantaneous, but will become part of your ongoing work over time. In this section, we focus on building instruction *from* and *with* the CCSS. As noted in Section I, building with the CCSS in mind does not mean checking boxes for individual standards; it means integrating a careful examination of the CCSS with the contexts and practices of our classrooms, always putting students at the center. The chapters in this section offer three approaches to this process of building: individual, collaborator, and advocate.

- *Individual*—There *are* things that you individually can do to keep students at the center of your work. In this section we discuss how you can read the CCSS document to help you plan instruction with the CCSS.

- *Collaborator*—We invite you also to think about how to collaborate with colleagues in planning and assessing with the CCSS, especially within and across grade levels.

- *Advocate*—In this section, we explore how you can use your knowledge about the CCSS and their language, along with your collaborative efforts, to advocate for the professional supports that will help you advance your students' learning needs.

Rest assured that like a marathoner in training, you cannot be expected to successfully tackle all three of these roles expertly as you begin your journey with the CCSS. Nor do we share these three roles to argue that you need to consider them sequentially or even fully. As you well know and as our experiences suggest, this process will be inherently like conditioning for a marathon. There will likely be great strides forward, plateaus, and at times struggles. But as the vignette teachers in this book illustrate, with the support of others near and far, holding the vision for what *can* be will sustain and affirm where you are headed.

Individual Considerations:
Keeping Students at the Center

5

I n reading this book, you have already begun considering how the CCSS pose new challenges that suggest you rethink and shift instruction. Reassure yourself that the CCSS do not have to call into question quality teaching practices, NCTE principles, and research. But the CCSS may ask you to rethink the complexity of *what* you teach. The charts at the end of each vignette chapter are a beginning effort to illustrate *how* and *why* we can and should be concerned about helping students negotiate increasingly complex learning tasks and texts; additionally, this chapter will help further articulate *how* you can plan with this goal in mind.

Reading the CCSS Document

The first step will be for you to individually negotiate and understand how the organization of the CCSS document requires close attention to detail. As we mentioned in Section I, the CCSS are grouped first by strands: K–5 and 6–12. These strands share strand sets, or College and Career Readiness Anchor Standards, in reading, writing, speaking and listening, and language. There are ten reading, ten writing, six speaking and listening, and six language Anchor Standards in each strand. Each Anchor Standard is then further detailed in grade-specific standards. The Anchor Standard is the foundation of the grade-specific standards, but the grade-specific standards include more specific language to further describe what the expectation is for students in each grade; therefore, there are some grade-specific standards that include sub-standards with numerals that further delineate such details. You will also notice that the CCSS focus a great deal on the kinds of reading students encounter across the school day, spelling out reading expectations for literature and informational texts. And at the K–5 level, the CCSS also include foundational skills standards.

An example of how this organization plays out in grades 3–5 may be helpful in explaining further. You'll note in Figure 5.1 an example of how you can read the CCSS for further specificity about grade-level distinctions using the first heading and Anchor Standard for reading.

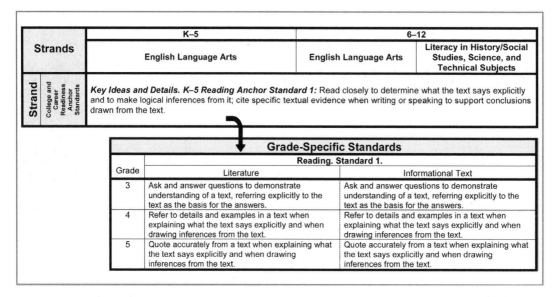

Strands	K–5	6–12	
	English Language Arts	English Language Arts	Literacy in History/Social Studies, Science, and Technical Subjects
Strand — College and Career Readiness Anchor Standards	**Key Ideas and Details. K–5 Reading Anchor Standard 1:** Read closely to determine what the text says explicitly and to make logical inferences from it; cite specific textual evidence when writing or speaking to support conclusions drawn from the text.		

	Grade-Specific Standards	
	Reading. Standard 1.	
Grade	Literature	Informational Text
3	Ask and answer questions to demonstrate understanding of a text, referring explicitly to the text as the basis for the answers.	Ask and answer questions to demonstrate understanding of a text, referring explicitly to the text as the basis for the answers.
4	Refer to details and examples in a text when explaining what the text says explicitly and when drawing inferences from the text.	Refer to details and examples in a text when explaining what the text says explicitly and when drawing inferences from the text.
5	Quote accurately from a text when explaining what the text says explicitly and when drawing inferences from the text.	Quote accurately from a text when explaining what the text says explicitly and when drawing inferences from the text.

FIGURE 5.1: Reading the CCSS with an example.

When you read the CCSS document, we encourage you to read for these distinctions between grade-specific standards. This will help you identify *what* students in the grade(s) you teach will be expected to enact to demonstrate proficiency.

Keeping Students at the Center

Reading the CCSS document with an eye toward distinguishing *what* students at the grade level(s) you teach will be expected to enact will help you keep your commitment to students at the center of your instructional decision making. Figure 5.2 illustrates how the multiple factors teachers consider when planning instruction speak to one another through teachers' knowledge of and interaction with students. As a teacher, all of your work with students happens in close relation to the context in which you teach, including your school and local community. So your students' needs, abilities, and interests—both individually and collectively—inform your decisions about planning for, enacting, and assessing instruction.

Keeping students at the center will enable you to prioritize what to attend to first and why. Furthermore, keeping students at the center may also empower you to utilize the CCSS mandate to advocate for your students' unique learning needs, as we discuss later in Chapter 7. Our collective teaching experiences across the country suggest challenges are inherent to good teaching—whether a result of the CCSS or

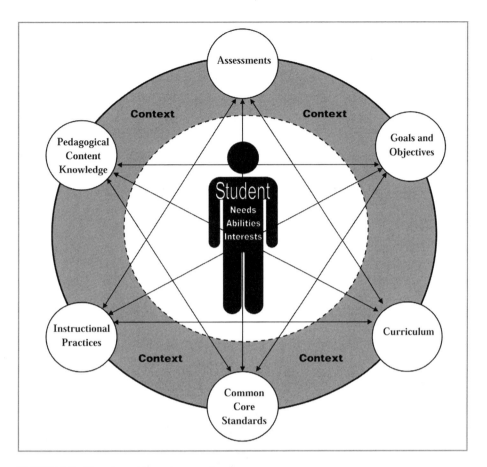

FIGURE 5.2: Planning with students at the center.

not—but foregrounding student learning needs, abilities, and interests provides a useful and necessary lens through which to interpret and implement the CCSS. No matter the pathway you choose to begin, as Figure 5.2 illustrates, your students provide the map for planning and journeying with the CCSS.

Instruction that keeps students at the center often begins by asking what knowledge is available about the needs, abilities, and interests of student learners, and applying this knowledge to instructional decisions made about goals and objectives, curriculum, the CCSS, instructional practices, pedagogical content knowledge, and assessment. Figure 5.3 contains the types of questions you might ask yourself as you begin to consider the knowledge you have about students and how this can shape your instructional decisions in response to the CCSS. Answering the questions in Figure 5.3 also involves careful consideration of your teaching context in relation to what you know about your students by asking about the community, family and home cultures, out-of-school experiences, and school and district culture that influence your students' schooling experiences and your instructional decision making.

Figure 5.4 provides a list of these questions that you can use as a beginning point for instructional planning. Your answers to these questions will help you enact teaching practices that support students' growing ability to make meaning of increasingly complex texts and enact increasingly complicated learning tasks. This approach, essential to the CCSS, can be described as spiraling instruction, and it's the approach that the vignette teachers you've read about use; in the following pages, we detail how this approach can help guide your individual planning for the students in your classroom.

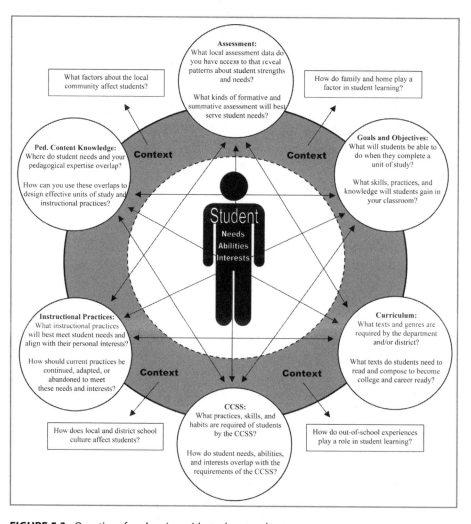

FIGURE 5.3: Questions for planning with students at the center.

What do I know about my **students** that supports my planning?

- Their needs –

- Their abilities –

- Their interests –

- Including:
    - Their home and heritage languages –

    - The funds of knowledge they bring from their homes and local communities –

    - The literacies students bring into the classroom –

Your Local Context

What factors about the local community affect students?

How do family and home play a factor in student learning?

How do out-of-school experiences play a role in student learning?

How does local and district school culture affect students?

FIGURE 5.4: Questions for planning template.

Assessment	Goals and Objectives
What local assessment data do you have access to that reveal patterns about student strengths and needs?	What will students be able to do when they complete a unit of study?
What kinds of formative and summative assessment will best serve student needs?	What skills, practices, and knowledge will students gain in your classroom?

Curriculum	CCSS
What texts and genres are required by the department and/or school district?	What practices, skills, and habits are required of students by the CCSS?
What texts do students need to read and compose to become college and career ready?	How do student needs, abilities, and interests overlap with the requirements of the CCSS?

Instructional Practices	Pedagogical Content Knowledge
What instructional practices will best meet student needs and align with their personal interests?	Where do student needs and your pedagogical expertise overlap?
How should current practices be continued, adapted, or abandoned to meet these needs and interests?	How can you use these overlaps to design effective units of study and instructional practices?

(Figure 5.4 continued)

Spiraling Instruction

As teachers, we know how difficult juggling the tasks of each day can be. Large class sizes, stacks of papers to grade, and limited collaborative and planning time often seem to get in the way of focusing fully on the needs of learners. At times, it may seem easier to plan lessons as lists of tasks just so you can make it smoothly through the day. In the past, we too have sometimes planned lessons in this way, using a monthly or a weekly calendar and filling the time with activities that aim in an unarticulated way at the objectives, skills, and practices we have in mind for students. Over time, however, we have come to view our planning differently, and this shift in our thinking and planning has actually increased the quality and complexity of the thinking and work of our students. In large part, this shift in our practice resulted from understanding how ELA instruction may differ from other content areas.

Unlike other content area instruction, which might be seen as building students' understandings and skills linearly, ELA learning can be seen as spiraling recursively. Research supports instructional planning that provides students with multiple opportunities to revisit concepts and enact their learning over time with increasing difficulty as more successful than planning and instruction that marches students through sets of activities and tasks. Planning this kind of instruction that spirals learning affords students opportunities to develop ELA understandings and skills within and across lessons, units of study, and courses.

As we've already discussed and as Figures 1.1 (see p. 7) and 5.1 help to illustrate, the CCSS embed text complexity within the Anchor Standards. Thus, increasing the complexity of tasks and reading is one way to spiral your instruction. Additionally, the grade-level-specific standards grouped around the same Anchor Standards can prove helpful in that they point out specific skills and practices students can work on in a particular grade level and suggest the expectation that students will add to and refine these skills as they move from one grade to the next. Spiraling instruction within grade levels is often referred to as horizontal alignment whereas spiraling instruction across grade levels is often referred to as vertical alignment. The organization of the CCSS, as outlined in Figure 1.1, can help you consider how to plan and align ELA instruction horizontally and vertically. Below, we'll focus on how you can plan instruction that spirals in your own classroom, but in Chapter 6, we'll return to this idea of horizontal and vertical alignment through a discussion of collaboration.

Planning Units of Study

Connections

Units of study, in the chapters that follow, refers not to the teaching of specific texts, but instead to designing groups of tasks, activities, and assessments that seek to meet an articulated set of goals, objectives, essential questions, themes, or genres.

Identifying how to begin planning units of study that spiral ELA instruction and meet the CCSS demands can feel like a daunting task. But after identifying the CCSS grade-specific expectations as well as your local approaches to asking students to demonstrate the learning and skills these expectations outline, you'll be ready to consider planning units.

Whether you are designing for the first time or revisiting previously taught units of study with your students' needs as the primary lens for shaping your instruction, there are multiple ways that you might choose to develop your units of study. The following list highlights some of the overarching approaches other teachers have chosen to guide the development of their units of study:

- *Thematic*—around themes that ask students to grapple with shared human experiences (e.g., loss, love, courage, heroism, empathy)

- *Essential questions*—around questions worthy of students' attention without easy right or wrong answers that ask students to seek understanding to act with resolve; many of these questions illuminate what it means to be human, how humans choose to respond to pressing issues, and ask students to wrestle with uncertainty and complexity (e.g., Under what circumstances are people justified in questioning authority? What is the cost of progress? Why is literature worthy of study?)

- *Genre study*—around particular genres or multigenres that offer students opportunities to study literature within the genre as fulcrum texts for students' writing in and speaking about the genre (e.g., narrative, short story, poetry, drama, essay, website)

None of these approaches is inherently better than the others. Rather, we suggest that whichever approach you choose, you can begin with student learning needs to spiral instruction and therefore learning toward further complexity. For example, if you wanted to organize your units thematically, you might begin using answers to Figure 5.4 questions to identify a theme that you know your students will find engaging and relevant as they read and write texts around the theme throughout the unit. Reading Anchor Standard 9 deals specifically with thematic understanding, so you can ask students to wrestle with theme in each unit (in addition to targeting other standards) by building on the expectations from a previous unit. Through this process, students will have to apply prior learning to a new theme and texts with new, more complex skills, strategies, and thinking.

Choosing Resources

With an organizational scheme in mind, in the early stages of unit planning, teachers often consider the texts they will use in a unit. We recognize that many districts or schools have adopted core texts or fulcrum texts that serve as the foundation of particular units of study. Identifying these and other resources in support of a unit's focus that meets the CCSS demands is an important consideration. As our earlier discussions in Section I affirmed, it will be important to also consider when choosing resources that the CCSS do encourage the unification of ELA strand sets (reading, writing, speaking and listening, and language) so that each unit of study integrates standards from each strand set (see Figure 1.1).

Connections
A useful and current definition of text clearly includes print materials such as novels, short stories, and poetry, but also expands to include other types of twenty-first-century documents such as newspaper and magazine articles, webpages, film and video, and even audio and sound clips. Expanding our notions of what counts as a text in classrooms is part of encouraging our students to develop multiple literacies.

We agree that teachers and students need greater access to a wider range of texts. Hopefully, the CCSS will raise awareness of why students would benefit from access to such materials, especially since the CCSS do raise awareness of the value of students' use of increasingly complex texts—both literature and informational. But we also acknowledge, based on our own experience, the range of choice that exists in different schools. For some of us, choice means selecting what was already available and finding free or reproducible alternatives when possible. For others, choice means the opportunity to order resources in support of unit objectives. There are unique challenges that each context poses. For those with little choice, considering how to help students meet the CCSS demands can seem nearly impossible.

Nonetheless, you can use a small sampling of various texts, even in different genres and modes, to help students navigate complex texts. *The Lightning Thief* and *The Fabled Fourth Graders of Aesop Elementary School* were used as read-alouds to support students' understandings of both the texts and the concepts being taught, while other texts, such as *Because of Winn-Dixie,* were used as part of guided reading to lessen the teacher support and increase student independence with scaffolding. As we learn more about text complexity and the ways to help our students navigate these texts, we recognize that we will all need to at least begin with what we have on our resource shelves and in our rooms. But the issue of pressing import may be less about what materials we have than what we do or, better yet, what we ask students to do. We can best focus our energies on going more deeply with fewer texts of greater complexity than on breadth and coverage. Resource choices should be made in conjunction with choices about unit objectives and goals that will help students meet the CCSS and more.

Beginning with the End in Mind:
Scaffolding Assessment throughout a Unit of Study

Because the CCSS are a set of grade-level expectations, they focus on outcomes. That is to say, the CCSS articulate what students should be able to do at the end of a particular grade. The CCSS as well as good unit design and planning suggest that we begin planning with the end in mind—that we keep omnipresent in our minds and on paper the ultimate goal we have for students. Figure 5.5, the unit plan template, provides one frame for thinking through and logging your plans for a unit of study.

We suggest that once you've identified the focus for a particular unit of study, you begin by identifying the outcome of the unit or what students will be expected to do at the end of the unit. Your unit objectives and goals will help you articulate what learning or tasks students will be able to enact at the end of the unit. Put another way, you'll want to identify the summative assessment that you'll ask students to complete at the end of the unit. Summative assessments focus on reporting whether students

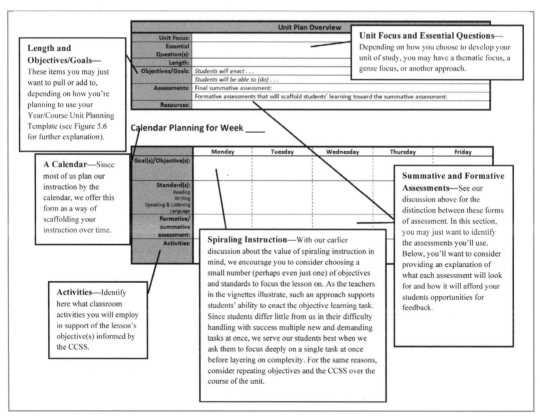

FIGURE 5.5: Unit plan template.

have met proficiency in demonstrating their ability to enact unit objectives. Often, summative assessments take the form of essays or presentations, but as NCTE notes on www.ncte.org/books/supp-students-3-5, there are many other forms of summative assessments.

Web 5.1

Although the CCSS are finally about what happens in the end, it is also important to note that the CCSS are not exhaustive. The CCSS need not limit the scope of your instruction. Yes, they set the minimum, but you can define the upper limits of your instruction and expectations for students as you plan instruction.

Similarly, it is critical to keep in mind that teacher-developed formative assessments will ultimately have the greatest influence on shaping the instruction and learning experiences that support students' ability to perform well on summative assessments. Multiple formative assessments strategically employed throughout a unit support ongoing learning and instruction. Katie's use of ABCD cards, Scott's use of the blog to monitor student responses to one another, and Kelley's use of teacher observation to select texts for instruction are all examples of how teachers employ formative assessment daily. As the NCTE Research Policy Brief "Fostering High-Quality Formative Assessment" details, high-quality formative assessments offer students *and* teachers more immediate feedback on students' ability to enact a specific learning task. This feedback helps students know how and why they can proceed in working to enact the task or in progressing toward the next task (part of spiraling instruction and learning). For teachers, formative assessments inform instructional decision making and interventions in helping to ensure that all students are able to meet proficiency on the summative assessment task(s).

Given the instructional and learning value of formative assessments, you will want to identify the formative assessments you'll include in your unit of study. The formative assessments you identify and design should help both you and your students identify where, when, and how to intervene in support of their learning and ability to enact the objectives, or learning tasks, throughout the unit. The formative assessments you choose should therefore come at critical points in the unit where you will be asking students to try out or enact new and difficult tasks. As you may already know or infer from the discussion thus far, formative assessments are not focused on grading students. Rather, formative assessments are focused on providing you and your students with feedback that will guide subsequent teaching and learning. This feedback will influence, as you help them to see, their later successful performance on the summative assessment. Collectively, the formative assessments you scaffold throughout the unit should help build students' ability and confidence in demonstrating proficiency on the latter summative assessment(s).

Figure 5.5 and the pull-out boxes (p. 78) offer further details about the type of planning thoughts you might want to record as you build or revise a unit of study with the end in mind.

Planning and Organizing Units across the Year or Semester

Identifying individual units of study cannot occur without simultaneously considering how multiple units of study progress across the year or semester (depending on the grade level). Teachers plan for instruction differently, but most attempt to help students gain deeper understandings by connecting concepts across time, disciplines, and experiences. Examples of this include Jalynn's use of social studies texts as the basis of mini-lessons and opportunities for summarizing; Kelley's efforts to help students understand author's purpose, a reading concept, from inside as a writer; and Dana's connection between drama and summary. The CCSS documents show many opportunities for connections between reading and writing, between content areas, and between concepts in fiction and nonfiction that could be useful in planning units of study.

As we have discussed, these considerations are a part of the spiraling that you can plan for across units of study. For example, teachers who choose a genre approach might begin with a personal narrative unit of study; students may review prior learning from a previous grade level and recall reading, thinking, and writing skills that will enable them to develop ideas for their narratives. In a later short-story unit, teachers might spiral students' learning by revisiting reading and thinking strategies in this new genre to explore with students how readers approach different kinds of texts. At the same time, teachers could introduce greater complexity in one or more of the thinking strategies they ask students to enact. And in terms of writing instruction, teachers might spiral instruction by building on earlier ways they invited students to develop ideas within a paragraph to consider how idea development works across paragraphs complicated by learning how this works in a new genre.

As you develop individual units of study in relation to other units, Figure 5.6 can serve as a tool for logging how you plan to spiral instruction within and across units of study. The pull-out boxes below offer further details about the type of planning thoughts you might want to record in each box.

Just as instruction spirals across a unit of study, so too does formative assessment. As students encounter new and increasingly difficult tasks, immediate feedback via formative assessments helps to build students' confidence and commitment to the task at hand. This is because the formative assessment helps students identify which areas they need to focus on and teachers can clarify misunderstanding. Formative assessments therefore boost students' learning across a unit of study; these formative assessments support students' improvement over time and ability to negotiate increasingly demanding tasks with independence.

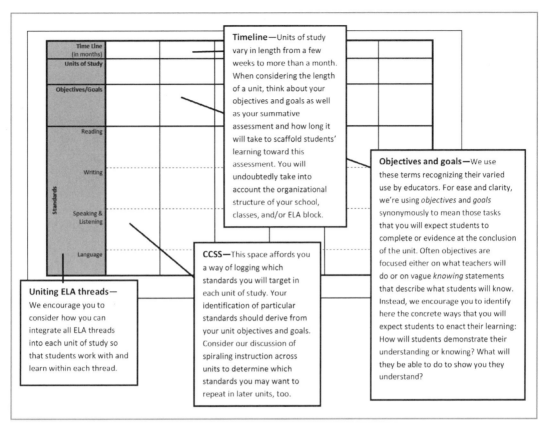

The template shown in the figure contains the following labeled callouts:

Timeline—Units of study vary in length from a few weeks to more than a month. When considering the length of a unit, think about your objectives and goals as well as your summative assessment and how long it will take to scaffold students' learning toward this assessment. You will undoubtedly take into account the organizational structure of your school, classes, and/or ELA block.

Objectives and goals—We use these terms recognizing their varied use by educators. For ease and clarity, we're using *objectives* and *goals* synonymously to mean those tasks that you will expect students to complete or evidence at the conclusion of the unit. Often objectives are focused either on what teachers will do or on vague *knowing* statements that describe what students will know. Instead, we encourage you to identify here the concrete ways that you will expect students to enact their learning: How will students demonstrate their understanding or knowing? What will they be able to do to show you they understand?

Uniting ELA threads—We encourage you to consider how you can integrate all ELA threads into each unit of study so that students work with and learn within each thread.

CCSS—This space affords you a way of logging which standards you will target in each unit of study. Your identification of particular standards should derive from your unit objectives and goals. Consider our discussion of spiraling instruction across units to determine which standards you may want to repeat in later units, too.

The template columns/rows are labeled: Time Line (in months), Units of Study, Objectives/Goals, Standards (Reading, Writing, Speaking & Listening, Language), CCSS.

FIGURE 5.6: Year/course unit planning template.

The chapters included in Section II provide a useful tool for thinking as you consider planning your own units of study. We do not offer them as packages to adopt; after all, such an approach might not take into consideration the unique contextual factors influencing your decision making, including, most notably, what you know about your students.

6

Working Collaboratively to Enact the CCSS

. . . .

As we have mentioned throughout the book, planning and teaching are collaborative processes strengthened with the support of colleagues. In Chapter 5, we discussed how your ongoing journey with the CCSS will centrally involve the students in your classroom, but your ability to positively affect student learning is largely influenced by the relationships you foster with colleagues as well. In this chapter, we suggest ways that teachers can work collaboratively to support one another and thereby their students.

Collaborate on Literacy across the Curriculum

The teachers' voices represented in this book and our ongoing conversations with colleagues across the nation reveal just how imperative collaborative efforts to understand and enact the CCSS are to the sustainability of our joint efforts. Many teachers—and administrators—are surprised to learn that the CCSS themselves urge us toward such aims. As we discussed earlier in our overview of the CCSS document and in Section I, the CCSS argue on page 7 that students who are college and career ready ought to be able to respond to a range of disciplinary demands, tasks, audiences, and purposes for writing, reading, speaking, and listening. The CCSS's inclusion of College and Career Readiness Anchor Standards at the K–5 grade levels for literacy in history/social science, science, and technical subjects sends a strong message that *with* our colleagues in these other content areas we are jointly responsible for helping students navigate the range of these literacy demands. Therefore, the CCSS recognize what we ELA teachers have long understood: we alone cannot take on the burden of equipping students to become literate consumers and producers of *all* content area knowledge. When some teachers read on page 5 of the CCSS document that by eighth grade, 45 percent of the sum of students' reading should be literary and the other 55 percent informational, they assume that this means that

Web 6.1
Go online for other resources for building schoolwide literacy initiatives.

they will need to devote 55 percent of students' ELA course reading to informational texts. However, consistent with this literacy across the content areas focus, the CCSS footnote to the chart with these percentages indicates that these targets are representative of students' reading of diverse texts across courses throughout their school day. Similarly, the CCSS spell out that the sum of eighth-grade students' writing should include students' writing in ELA *and* non-ELA settings so that 35 percent of students' writing across courses will be to persuade, 35 percent to explain, and 30 percent to convey experience. It is therefore important for us to work with colleagues across content areas to determine how best to jointly support students' reading and writing across the school day in the range of their coursework.

Look for Opportunities to Form Professional Learning Groups and Communities

Professional learning groups and communities are powerful locations for teacher growth, development, and collaboration. As you work collaboratively with your colleagues, grade-level band, and department, look for opportunities to initiate authentic, inquiry-driven professional learning communities. A professional learning group can be a place to house discussion about the CCSS, NCTE principles, NCTE policy briefs, NCTE Web seminars, or professional books. To help you begin imagining new ways to engage in collaboration at your school, we have provided a few possible suggestions. These various opportunities for collaboration can strengthen communities of learning as they address the CCSS.

- *Start a Teachers as Readers Book Group.* Some professional learning communities are designed as book clubs. Members read and discuss children's and young adults' literature along with professional texts.

Web 6.2

- *Take advantage of collaborative spaces.* Departmental meetings can be great places to work collaboratively with colleagues. In some schools, this will mean rethinking current views about departmental meetings. Often, with the best intentions, these spaces focus primarily on logistical issues with little support for teachers to draw on their own backgrounds and styles and embrace the strengths and needs of their students, but department meetings can be spaces where professional planning is grounded in a commitment to the autonomy of knowledgeable teachers who make decisions for and with their students. With such a view, department meetings can be places where teachers engage in professional study and reflection that supports growth in the company of colleagues who are wrestling with similar issues.

- *Attend national conferences.* Attending professional conferences is a fabulous way for teachers to find space and support for focused reflection. Through these experiences, teachers share their great work and learn from others in ways that will ultimately enhance successful teaching in their home districts and schools. Conferences support teachers by giving them opportunities to become intellectually reinvigorated by engaging with colleagues from across the country.

- *Seek out online forums.* Online forums are another space for reflection and growth. Participating in such forums, teachers gain insights from across the country as they have opportunities to share their work and learn from others' classrooms. With other teachers, they address challenges, pose questions, provide insight, and find new ideas about practice, materials, and other resources.

Web 6.3

Plan, Develop, and Assess with the CCSS

Connections

As these teachers' practices illustrate, the CCSS need not overshadow the particularities of the places in which we all teach.

The CCSS document details grade-specific expectations but questions about how students will be asked to demonstrate the standard-specific task of understanding are left to teachers' collective expertise. To be clear, the CCSS do not advocate for particular ELA pedagogy. Therefore, collaborating with colleagues in your school, district, region, and state can help you localize the CCSS; together you can interpret the CCSS language and plan to enact the CCSS grade-level expectations in the ways most responsive to your local context.

Identify Grade-Level Distinctions

Figure 6.1 builds on our conversations about how to read the CCSS document for grade-level differences. This model can help you and your colleagues extend your initial individual thinking about horizontal and vertical alignment in relation to the CCSS document. The figure serves as a tool for articulating how you will ask students to demonstrate grade-level distinctions and what they will look like in your classrooms. By noting in the boxes what language is added or changed in the progression from grade to grade and how this language might translate to instructional choices and student activities, Figure 6.1 can be used on three levels:

- Level 1: to identify the CCSS Anchor Standards distinctions across grade levels
- Level 2: to identify the learning tasks that students will need to enact to demonstrate proficiency in meeting each standard

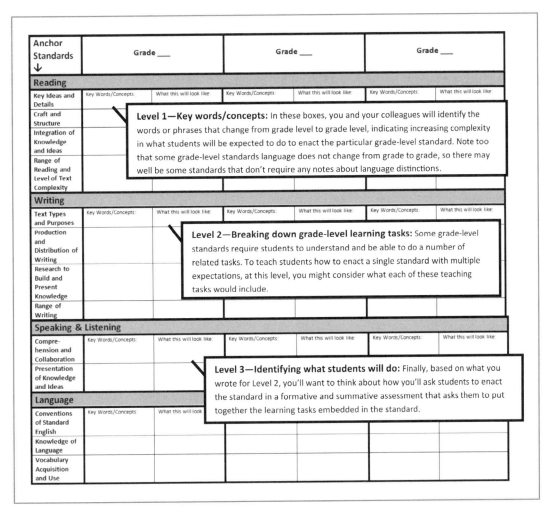

The table template:

Anchor Standards ↓	Grade ___		Grade ___		Grade ___	
Reading						
Key Ideas and Details	Key Words/Concepts:	What this will look like:	Key Words/Concepts:	What this will look like:	Key Words/Concepts:	What this will look like:
Craft and Structure						
Integration of Knowledge and Ideas						
Range of Reading and Level of Text Complexity						
Writing						
Text Types and Purposes	Key Words/Concepts:	What this will look like:	Key Words/Concepts:	What this will look like:	Key Words/Concepts:	What this will look like:
Production and Distribution of Writing						
Research to Build and Present Knowledge						
Range of Writing						
Speaking & Listening						
Comprehension and Collaboration	Key Words/Concepts:	What this will look like:	Key Words/Concepts:	What this will look like:	Key Words/Concepts:	What this will look like:
Presentation of Knowledge and Ideas						
Language						
Conventions of Standard English	Key Words/Concepts:	What this will look				
Knowledge of Language						
Vocabulary Acquisition and Use						

Text box annotations within the figure:

Level 1—Key words/concepts: In these boxes, you and your colleagues will identify the words or phrases that change from grade level to grade level, indicating increasing complexity in what students will be expected to do to enact the particular grade-level standard. Note too that some grade-level standards language does not change from grade to grade, so there may well be some standards that don't require any notes about language distinctions.

Level 2—Breaking down grade-level learning tasks: Some grade-level standards require students to understand and be able to do a number of related tasks. To teach students how to enact a single standard with multiple expectations, at this level, you might consider what each of these teaching tasks would include.

Level 3—Identifying what students will do: Finally, based on what you wrote for Level 2, you'll want to think about how you'll ask students to enact the standard in a formative and summative assessment that asks them to put together the learning tasks embedded in the standard.

FIGURE 6.1: Grade-level distinctions planning template.

- Level 3: to identify what you'll ask your students to do to enact the CCSS articulated expectations. In this level, together you can identify common formative and summative assessments you might use within and/or across grade levels

You can therefore use this document three separate times or for three separate passes to examine and discuss each focus level. Or you could choose to focus on a single level that offers you a way to scaffold conversations with your colleagues. The textboxes help to explain how Figure 6.1 can be used at each level.

In Figure 6.2, we provide an example of how you might use this document at all three levels using Anchor Speaking and Listening Standard 4. The pull-outs highlight further thinking at each level of discussion.

It is important to note that this chart does not need to replace your existing tools and resources for mapping curriculum. Instead, it offers one way to help you think through the grade-level distinctions in conversations with others.

Plan Common Course or Grade-Level Instruction

Understanding the grade-level distinctions using Figure 6.1 might also encourage you to consider ways to plan instruction with others who teach the same course or grade level. You can focus together on integrating ELA threads as well. We encourage you to consider using Figures 5.5 and 5.6 to facilitate your discussions and plans with colleagues who teach the same grade level or course as well as department colleagues who can help you think about spiraling instruction from previous grades and courses for students.

Identify Common Texts

Meeting in grade level, course teams, or departments to develop units around core, or fulcrum, texts can be a useful way to align instruction with the CCSS. Using common texts can be a way to reorient your conversations toward students' ability to enact learning tasks and you can share common experiences to adapt instruction while still feeling at liberty to pick context and texture texts. Together you can ask questions as you begin planning about which texts to choose and why:

- What young adult novels, poems, nonfiction articles, or other texts could supplement fulcrum texts?
- How can we incorporate other ELA threads in our discussion of and writing about chosen texts?
- How can we integrate digital technology or multimodal opportunities for students to enact the CCSS learning tasks as they read and compose texts?
- How can we support struggling or reluctant readers with the chosen fulcrum texts?

Anchor Standards	Grade 3		Grade 4	
Speaking				
Presentation of Knowledge and Ideas #4	Key Words/Concepts: **1st Level—** Report on a topic or text, tell a story, or recount an experience with appropriate facts and relevant, descriptive details, speaking clearly at an understandable pace.	What this will look like: **2nd Level—** • Present in different ways, such as telling stories or giving information. • Use relevant details that stay on topic. • Deliver ideas clearly and at a speed that the audience can understand. **3rd Level—** *In Units 1–3 in response to the core text:* • Recount an experience similar to one a character from the text experienced, comparing and contrasting your experience with the character's experience.	Key Words/Concepts: **1st Level—** *In addition to 3:* • Recount and report in an organized manner. • Support main ideas or themes.	What this will look like: **2nd Level—** *In addition to 3:* • Identify a main idea, theme, or message that is emerging from the presentation. • Use supporting details to back up or elaborate on the theme or main idea. • Illustrate the ability to structure a presentation in an organized way. **3rd Level—** *In Units 1–3 in response to the core text:* • Recount an experience similar to one a character from the text experienced, identifying how the character's experience and yours were thematically similar, using a compare/contrast organizational structure to present your experience.

Level 1—Here it may be easier to begin with the first grade level by writing the full standard or by listing key words. Because of the density of this standard, we chose to list the entire standard.

Level 1—In each subsequent grade level, you might just add what other items are mentioned or in some other way indicate differences from the earlier grade(s).

Level 2—We thought about each of the different learning tasks that students would need to enact to demonstrate successful proficiency in meeting this standard.

Level 3—You'll notice that we have just begun this level. We are noting what units might take into account which learning tasks. Remember that not every unit need expect students to enact all of the learning tasks for each standard. This is part of the power of spiraled instruction, where you can return to standards with increasing complexity over the semester or year or course.

FIGURE 6.2: Grade-level distinctions example.

Select and Enact a New Teaching Strategy

Beyond planning together, trying out a new teaching strategy in your classroom can be easier when you do it along with one or two other teachers. The CCSS invite teachers to study how particular instructional practices support student learning and ability to demonstrate proficiency in meeting and exceeding the CCSS expectations. If your building has a literacy specialist or lead literacy teacher, you can ask him or her to help you plan and give you feedback or you can build a study group focused on action research with other colleagues. Once you try out the new strategy, evaluate the results using joint learning goals and objectives, and work together to tweak and repeat. Your group can also share your results with your grade-level group or department.

Develop Common Assessments

Level 3 of Figure 6.1, as the example in Figure 6.2 begins, invites you to consider how you might collaboratively identify, develop, and adapt common formative and summative assessments within grade levels or courses taught by more than one teacher. Some teacher learning communities use common assessments to review their instruction as well as students' work throughout units of study. Because they share the assessments and the language, making adjustments to instruction in the midst of units and in relation to future units becomes a shared responsibility. In this way, these teachers remain ever responsive to their students' learning needs and ultimately to their students' ability to enact unit learning tasks that demonstrate their ability to meet the CCSS demands.

Share Ideas Online with Colleagues Near and Far

We encourage you to share your efforts and ideas in online professional forums and with your colleagues in your professional learning communities. Because all of the

Web 6.4

figures and charts throughout this book are also available for your use and adaptation on www.ncte.org/books/supp-students-3-5, we hope you will share your thinking related to, experiences using, and revision of these resources and about the CCSS more generally there. Supporting one another online in such a forum is one way to strengthen our ability to help students meet the CCSS demands and to remind ourselves that colleagues nationwide are negotiating similar challenges. You can also find interactive lesson plans at www.readwritethink.org, or contribute some of your own.

In a profession where we all largely perform the obligations and duties of our role as ELA teachers alone in our classrooms, it is critically important to remember that you are not alone in this effort to enact the CCSS. We hope the teachers you've met in Section II highlight the powerful potential of uniting with others who share the challenge of meeting the CCSS demands.

Becoming a Teacher Advocate

7

The teachers featured in Section II highlight powerful ways of leveraging the CCSS to shape instruction that meets students' needs and prepares them to contribute to a world we can only imagine today. These teachers, however, are but a few of the thousands of committed K–12 ELA teachers who share this goal, including you. Part of your strength and expertise as an ELA teacher and/or instructional leader is your ability to advocate for your own professional needs, and therefore your students' learning needs, in collaboration with others near and far. Your commitment to reading this book, to learning about how the CCSS intersect with your teaching practices, and to working with others to learn and plan together illustrates your concern for keeping students at the center.

Throughout this book we have discussed ways in which you can work individually and collaboratively to make sense of, put into perspective, and act in relation to the CCSS; in this brief final section we invite you to begin considering how you can work to advocate locally, within your state, and even nationally in equally important small and large ways for the support that will enable you to sustain the professional learning and practices in support of students' needs. Below we highlight by building on earlier conversations ways that you can begin this advocacy work.

Advocate for Yourself by Committing to Continued Professional Growth

Every teacher knows that professional autonomy is not a given. When discussing standards or other guidelines, it is important to be alert to tendencies to look at the CCSS as a means to homogenize ways of teaching and students' pathways to learning. At the same time, teachers have a responsibility to meet their side of the bargain. As teachers, we cannot claim the right to autonomy without committing to ongoing, focused professional growth.

Advocate for Your Students by Using Knowledge of Your Context to Design Instruction

Rigid interpretations of standards often lead to the imposition of rigid pacing guides and scripted programs that tell teachers what to do and say. Scripted programs limit what teachers can do in their classrooms by failing to draw on their professional knowledge. Work together in schools and districts to ensure that standards are used knowledgeably and responsibly so that policies never deny teachers their ability to use their professional knowledge.

Advocate for Instruction That Is Student Centered

We know that using the cultural heritages, orientations, and resources of ethnically and racially diverse students helps them learn. Seek, find, celebrate, and utilize the rich languages and literacies that exist in the homes and communities of your students. Students also bring diverse learning styles and enormous variations and abilities; consider these in developing instruction. Fill your classroom and the halls of your schools with wide varieties of languages, literacies, and abilities. Teach about them and teach through them. Because our choice in resources ought to be guided by the overarching goals and purposes that guide our planning units of study, we can best persuade internal and external stakeholders about the worth and necessity of such resources when we can also provide a compelling rationale. The best rationale centers on student achievement.

Advocate for the Use of Locally Developed Formative Assessments

It is critically important to recognize your professional expertise in developing formative assessments that speak with specificity to your students' learning needs. You know the local needs of your students and the community that supports their learning in and out of school. Therefore, you and your colleagues are best suited to design, implement, and adjust the formative assessments that will best enable your students to meet the demands of the CCSS. Speaking with colleagues both near and far will enable you to speak compellingly with local and national stakeholders about how your locally designed, implemented, and adjusted formative assessments best meet your students' needs and are still responsive to the CCSS.

Advocate for Your Students by Contributing to Larger Professional Communities

When our days are consumed by the immediate needs of our students and colleagues, it can feel overwhelming to think of joining other colleagues from afar. Alternately, you may wonder what you have to contribute to a larger professional community beyond your school or district. But you can rest assured that the time and energy necessary to do so are well worth it and less extensive than you might think. You do have a lot to share with others; your experiences are worthy of others' attention. And professional organizations such as NCTE are a renewing space to remind yourself of this and to find solace and empowerment, especially as you meet the challenges of the CCSS.

We share your concern about the onslaught of attacks against teachers, including ELA teachers, by those who question our professional knowledge. Connecting with others near and far to give voice to your expertise is one amazingly powerful way to begin speaking back persuasively. And in this time of the CCSS, we believe in the work illustrated by the teachers featured in Section II and similarly enacted by teachers like you across this country. Your teaching practices and efforts to keep students at the center illustrate that the CCSS can be leveraged toward powerful ends by those of us who do the work that matters daily with the students in our lives. By connecting with one another locally, regionally, and nationally, we have the power to influence what the CCSS will become by joining the conversation. But it's more than just connecting. By equipping ourselves with the knowledge that comes from observing the CCSS deeply and from centering our CCSS-informed instruction on our knowledge of local contexts, we can join with teachers locally, nationally, and internationally in building instructional practices that will enable students to develop the habits that lead to becoming flexible, adaptive readers, writers, thinkers, and doers who are ready to meet the challenges of the twenty-first century.

Appendix A

Resources

Following is a consolidation of professional resources provided throughout and in support of the issues and concepts discussed in this text. These resources could serve educators' ongoing discussions, study groups, and individual inquiries equally well.

Topic	Resource
Guided reading and small-group instruction	Biddulph, J. (2002). *The Guided Reading Approach: Theory and Practice.* Wellington, New Zealand: Learning Media. Retrieved from *http://www .thebiddulphgroup.net.nz/Portals/0/Other/GuidedReading2002.pdf*
	Boushey, G., & Moser, J. (2006). *The daily five: Fostering literacy independence in the elementary grades.* Portland, ME: Stenhouse.
	Clark, B. M., & Ramsey, M. E. (1973). Why small group instruction? *NASSP Bulletin, 57*(369): 64–71.
	Fountas, I. C., & Pinnell, G. S. (1996). *Guided reading: Good first teaching for all children.* Portsmouth, NH: Heinemann.
	Fountas, I. C., & Pinnell, G. S. (2001). *Guiding readers and writers grades 3–6: Teaching comprehension, genre and content literacy.* Portsmouth, NH: Heinemann.
	Fountas, I. C., & Pinnell, G. S. (2006). *Teaching for comprehending and fluency: Thinking, talking, and writing about reading, K–8.* Portsmouth, NH: Heinemann.
	McLaughlin, M., & Allen, M. B. (2002). *Guided comprehension: A teaching model for grades 3–8.* Newark, DE: International Reading Association.
Scaffolding literacy learning: Demonstration, read-aloud, and independent reading	Duffy, G. G. (2002). The case for direct explanation of strategies. In C. C. Block & M. Pressley (Eds.), *Comprehension Instruction: Research-based best practices* (pp. 28–41). New York: Guildford Press.
	Duke, N. K., & Pearson, P. D. (2002). Effective practices for developing reading comprehension. In A. E. Farstrup & S. J. Samuels (Eds.), *What research has to say about reading instruction* (3rd ed., pp. 205–242). Newark, DE: International Reading Association.
	Guthrie, J. T., Schafer, W., Wang, Y. Y., & Afflerbach, P. (1995). Relationships of instruction to amount of reading: An exploration of social, cognitive, and instructional connections. *Reading Research Quarterly, 30*(1), 8–25.

Topic	Resource
Scaffolding literacy learning: Demonstration, read-aloud, and independent reading *(continued)*	Harvey, S., & Goudvis, A. (2007). *Strategies that work: Teaching comprehension to enhance understanding.* Portland, ME: Stenhouse.
	Katz, C. A. (with Polkoff, L., & Durvitz, D.). (2005). Shhh . . . I'm reading: Scaffolded independent-level reading. *School Talk, 10*(2), 1–3.
	Kucan, L., & Beck, I. L. (1997). Thinking aloud and reading comprehension research: Inquiry, instruction, and social interaction. *Review of Educational Research, 67*(3), 271–299.
	Maria, K., & Hathaway, K. (1993). Using think alouds with teachers to develop awareness of reading strategies. *Journal of Reading, 37*(1), 12–18.
	Morrow, L. M. (2003). Motivating lifelong voluntary readers. In J. Flood, D. Lapp, J. R. Squire, & J. M. Jensen (Eds.), *Handbook of research on teaching the English language arts* (2nd ed., pp. 857–67). Mahwah, NJ: Erlbaum.
	Pearson, P. D., & Gallagher, M. C. (1983). The instruction of reading comprehension. *Contemporary Educational Psychology, 8*(3), 317–344.
	Szymusiak, K., Sibberson, F., & Koch, L. (2008). *Beyond leveled books: Supporting early and transitional readers in grades K–5* (2nd ed.). Portland, ME: Stenhouse.
	Taberski, S. (1998). What's your role during independent reading? *Instructor, 107*(5), 32–34.
	Trelease, J. (2001). *The read-aloud handbook* (5th ed.). New York: Penguin.
	Wood, K. D., Lapp, D., Flood, J., & Taylor, D. B. (2008). *Guiding readers through text: Strategy guides for new times.* Newark, DE: International Reading Association.
Blogging and using technology	Kitsis, S. (2010). The virtual cycle: When a teacher added online discussion, her literature circles thrived. *Educational Leadership, 68*(1), 50–54.
	Richardson, W. (2006). *Blogs, wikis, podcasts, and other powerful web tools for classrooms.* Thousand Oaks, CA: Corwin Press.
	Zuger, S. (2010). How it's done: Yes—student blogs allowed! *Tech and Learning, 30*(9), 18.
Formative assessment	Black, P., Harrison, C. Lee, C., Marshall, B., & Wiliam, D. (2004). Working inside the black box: Assessment for learning in the classroom. *Phi Delta Kappan, 86*(1), 8–21.
	Clarke, S. (2001). *Unlocking formative assessment: Practical strategies for enhancing pupils' learning in the primary classroom.* London: Hodder and Stoughton Educational.
	Fisher, D., & Frey, N. (2007). *Checking for understanding: Formative assessment techniques for your classroom.* Alexandria, VA: Association for Supervision and Curriculum Development.
	Fisher, D., Grant, M., Frey, N., & Johnson, C. (2007–2008). Taking formative assessment schoolwide. *Educational Leadership, 65*(4), 64–68.
	Owocki, G., & Goodman, Y. (2002*). Kidwatching: Documenting children's literacy development.* Portsmouth, NH: Heinemann.
	Sibberson, F., & Szymusiak, K. (2008). *Day-to-day assessment in the reading workshop: Making informed instructional decisions in grades 3–6.* New York: Scholastic.
	Stiggins, R. J., Arter, J. A, Chappuis, J., & Chappuis, S. (2004). *Classroom assessment for student learning: Doing it right—using it well.* Portland, OR: Assessment Training Institute.
	Wiliam, D., Lee, C., Harrison, C., & Black, P. (2004). Teachers developing assessment for learning: Impact on student achievement. *Assessment in Education: Principles, Policy and Practice, 11*(1), 49–65.

Topic	Resource
Student talk	Allington, R. L. (2002). What I've learned about effective reading instruction from a decade of studying exemplary elementary classroom teachers. *Phi Delta Kappan, 83*(10), 740–747.
	Calkins, L. M. (2001). *The Art of Teaching Reading*. New York: Longman.
	Gambrell, L. B. (1996). What research reveals about discussion. In L. B. Gambrell & J. F. Almasi (Eds.), *Lively discussions! Fostering engaged reading* (pp. 39–51). Newark, DE: International Reading Association.
Classroom culture	Allington, R. L., & Johnston, P. H. (2000). *What do we know about effective fourth-grade teachers and their classrooms?* (CELA Research Report No. 13010). Albany: National Research Center on English Learning and Achievement, State University of New York.
	Eeds, M., & Wells, D. (1989). Grand conversations: An exploration of meaning construction in literature study groups. *Research in the Teaching of English, 23*(1), 4–29.
	Marzano, R. J., Pickering, D. J., & Pollack, J. E. (2001). *Classroom instruction that works: Research-based strategies for increasing student achievement.* Alexandria, VA: Association for Supervision and Curriculum Development.
	Miller, D. (2008). *Teaching with intention: Defining beliefs, aligning practice, taking action, K–5.* Portland, ME: Stenhouse.
Units of study	Akhavan, N. L. (2004). *How to align literacy instruction, assessment, and standards: And achieve results you never dreamed possible.* Portsmouth, NH: Heinemann.
	Ray, K. W. (2006). *Study Driven: A framework for planning units of study in the writing workshop.* Portsmouth, NH: Heinemann.
Struggling readers	Beers. K. (2003). *When kids can't read: What teachers can do.* Portsmouth, NH: Heinemann.
	Lyons, C. A. (2003). *Teaching struggling readers: How to use brain-based research to maximize learning.* Portsmouth, NH: Heinemann.
	Pinnell, G. S., & Fountas, I. C. (2009). *When readers struggle: Teaching that works.* Portsmouth, NH: Heinemann.
	Taylor, B. M., Pearson, P. D., Clark, K. F., & Walpole, S. (1999). *Beating the odds in teaching all children to read* (CIERA Report No. 2-006). Ann Arbor: Center for the Improvement of Early Reading Achievement, University of Michigan.
Collaboration and professional development	Darling-Hammond, L., & Bransford, J. (Eds). (2005). *Preparing teachers for a changing world: What teachers should learn and be able to do.* San Francisco, CA: Jossey Bass.
	DuFour, R., DuFour, R., & Eaker, R. (2008). *Revisiting professional learning communities at work: New insights for improving schools.* Bloomington, IN: Solution Tree.

Appendix B

NCTE Principles

Throughout this book, there have been references to the NCTE principles that guide inspiring and effective teachers such as those featured in the vignettes. Drawn from research and based on classroom practices that foster student learning, these principles provide the foundation on which excellent teaching and enhanced student learning is built. This section includes explanations of NCTE principles about several areas of instruction—reading, writing, speaking and listening, and language—along with principles on formative assessment, teaching English language learners, 21st century literacies, and the role of teachers as decision makers in planning and implementing instruction. This last is the overarching principle under which all the others are clustered because it speaks to the heart of teacher work.

The principles in this appendix represent a compilation of work created and endorsed by NCTE, much of which can be found and is referenced on the NCTE website. As you think about ways to begin planning and shifting your instruction to align with the CCSS, use this document as a reference and resource, grounding your instruction, as well, in established, research-based NCTE principles. Each set of principles is organized into two categories: what NCTE knows about learners and learning, and what that knowledge means for teachers in the classroom.

NCTE Principles Regarding Teachers as Decision Makers

A number of NCTE documents affirm the role of teachers as decision makers. Among the most recent are the 2005 "Features of Literacy Programs: A Decision-Making Matrix," produced by the Commission on Reading; the 2008 Resolution passed by the Board of Directors on Scripted Curricula; and the 2010 Resolution on Affirming the Role of Teachers and Students in Developing Curriculum.

Both the CCSS and NCTE agree that teachers' professional judgment and experience should shape the way that the goals inherent in the CCSS will be reached. Common agreement on what students should be able to accomplish leaves ample room for teachers to make decisions about the materials and strategies that will be used in the classroom. Teachers are not simply implementation agents for the CCSS; rather, they are active shapers of schoolwide plans that will enable students to reach the goals of these or any standards.

The journeys recounted in this book demonstrate that teachers work, learn, and plan most effectively when they collaborate with their colleagues. Indeed, research shows that teaching teams are a vital unit of school change and improvement.

What we know about teaching as a profession:

Working in teams allows teachers to design and share goals and strategies, strengthens the foundation for informed decision making, and contributes to participation in more broadly based communities of practice. Teaching teams bring together teachers, administrators, and other educators to:

- Develop and assess curricula
- Assess and become more knowledgeable about student learning
- Design and support activities that enhance professional practice
- Apply cross-disciplinary perspectives to curriculum design, assessment, and professional growth
- Conduct collective inquiry into the learning and teaching environment
- Connect to parents and the community

We also know that teaching is a professional endeavor, and that teachers are active problem solvers and decision makers in the classroom. As professionals, teachers and students benefit from sustained and empowering professional development for teachers.

What this means for educators:

- Administrators and teacher leaders should provide for systematic professional development as an essential component of successful school reform. Teachers who have opportunities for quality professional development are best able to help students learn.

- We need to collectively define teacher effectiveness as professional practice that uses deep content knowledge, effective pedagogy, authentic formative assessments, connections with parents and communities, sustained reflection, and research-based practices to engage students and help them learn.

- Schools should support a comprehensive literacy policy as described in the Literacy Education for All, Results for the Nation (LEARN) Act that requires a sustained investment in literacy learning and instruction from birth through grade 12 and empowers teachers to design and select formative assessments and lessons.

NCTE Principles Regarding Reading Instruction

The original version of this NCTE Guideline, titled "On Reading, Learning to Read, and Effective Reading Instruction: An Overview of What We Know and How We Know It," can be found on NCTE's website at http://www.ncte.org/positions /statements/onreading and was authored by The Commission on Reading of the National Council of Teachers of English.

As the teachers in this volume have demonstrated, reading instruction consumes a lot of our attention in the classroom. The creators of the CCSS have acknowledged the importance of literacy for twenty-first-century learners by including standards for literacy instruction across content areas; indeed, as reading materials become more diverse and complex in this digital age, we need to prepare our students to encounter different types of texts in different situations.

What we know about reading and learning to read:

- Reading is a complex and purposeful sociocultural, cognitive, and linguistic process in which readers simultaneously use their knowledge of spoken and written language, their knowledge of the topic of the text, and their knowledge of their culture to construct meaning with text.
- Readers read for different purposes.
- As children learn to read continuous text, they use their intuitive knowledge of spoken language and their knowledge of the topic to figure out print words in text.
- The more children read, the better readers they become.
- Children read more when they have access to engaging, age-appropriate books, magazines, newspapers, computers, and other reading materials. They read more on topics that interest them than on topics that do not interest them.
- Reading supports writing development and writing supports reading development.
- All readers use their life experiences, their knowledge of the topic, and their knowledge of oral and written language to make sense of print.
- Readers continue to grow in their ability to make sense of an increasing variety of texts on an increasing variety of topics throughout their lives.

What this means for teachers of reading:

- Teachers should know their students as individuals, including their interests, their attitudes about reading, and their school, home, and community experiences.
- Teachers should read to students daily using a variety of text types.

- Teachers should try to use a variety of instructional groupings, including whole-group, small-group, and individual instruction, to provide multiple learning experiences.
- Teachers should teach before-, during-, and after-reading strategies for constructing meaning of written language, including demonstrations and think-alouds.
- Teachers should provide specific feedback to students to support their reading development.
- Teachers should provide regular opportunities for students to respond to reading through discussion, writing, art, drama, storytelling, music, and other creative expressions.
- Teachers should provide regular opportunities for students to reflect on their learning.
- Teachers should gradually release instructional responsibility to support independent reading.
- Teachers need to reflect on their students' progress and their own teaching practices to make changes that meet the needs of students.

NCTE Principles Regarding the Teaching of Writing

The original version of this NCTE Guideline, titled "NCTE Beliefs about the Teaching of Writing," can be found on NCTE's website at http://www.ncte.org/positions/statements/writingbeliefs. It was originally authored by the Writing Study Group of the NCTE Executive Committee.

Just as the nature of and expectation for literacy has changed in the past century and a half, so has the nature of writing. Much of that change has been due to technological developments, from pen and paper, to typewriter, to word processor, to networked computer, to design software capable of composing words, images, and sounds. These developments not only expanded the types of texts that writers produce, but they also expanded immediate access to a wider variety of readers. The CCSS acknowledge this reality with standards that note the need for students to be able to use technology critically and effectively in their writing, but it is up to teachers to decide how to engage students with meaningful writing tasks that will enable them to meet the demands of our quickly changing society.

What we know about writing and learning to write:

- Everyone has the capacity to write, writing can be taught, and teachers can help students become better writers.
- People learn to write by writing.
- Writing is a process and a tool for thinking.
- Writing grows out of many different purposes.
- Conventions of finished and edited texts are important to readers and therefore to writers.
- Writing and reading are related.
- Literate practices are embedded in complicated social relationships.
- Composing occurs in different modalities and technologies.
- Assessment of writing involves complex, informed, human judgment.

What this means for teachers of writing:

- Writing instruction must include ample in-class and out-of-class opportunities for writing and should include writing for a variety of purposes and audiences.

- Instruction should be geared toward making sense in a life outside of school.

- Writing instruction must provide opportunities for students to identify the processes that work best for themselves as they move from one writing situation to another.

- Writing instruction must take into account that a good deal of workplace writing and other writing takes place in collaborative situations.

- It is important that teachers create opportunities for students to be in different kinds of writing situations, where the relationships and agendas are varied.

- Simply completing workbook or online exercises is inadequate.

- Students should have access to and experience in reading material that presents both published and student writing in various genres.

- Students should be taught the features of different genres *experientially*, not only explicitly.

- The teaching of writing should assume students will begin with the sort of language with which they are most at home and most fluent in their speech.

- Writing instruction must accommodate the explosion in technology from the world around us.

- Instructors must recognize the difference between formative and summative evaluation and be prepared to evaluate students' writing from both perspectives.

NCTE Principles Regarding
Speaking and Listening

NCTE principles on speaking and listening are articulated in "Guideline on the Essentials of English," which can be found at http://www.ncte.org/positions/statements/essentialsofenglish.

NCTE has a long history of supporting both instruction and assessment that integrates speaking and listening skills into the teaching of the English language arts, and the CCSS acknowledge the importance of speaking and listening in their Speaking and Listening Standards. Speaking refers to both informal speech, such as talking in small groups or participating in class discussions, and formal speech that results from composing and presenting a text. Listening means engaging in a complex, active process that serves a variety of purposes.

What we know about speaking and listening in school:

- Public speaking is consistently ranked as one of the greatest sources of anxiety for people of all ages, and students are no exception.
- Much of the work of the classroom is done through speaking and listening.
- Formal speaking can be extemporaneous, relying on detailed notes but no actual script, or text-based.
- If students spend discussion time competing for the attention of the teacher rather than listening and responding to peers, they will not benefit from the informal speech in the classroom.
- It can be difficult to evaluate listening.
- One of the advantages of speaking is that it can generate immediate response, and it is important to make full use of this feature.

What this means for teachers of speaking and listening:

- To ensure that all students have an opportunity to develop skills of informal speech, teachers should not depend exclusively on volunteers in class discussion.
- Strategies for broadening participation include having all students respond in writing and then asking each student to respond aloud, asking students to discuss in pairs and report to the class, or distributing "talk tokens" that students can turn in after a contribution to a class discussion.

- Teachers should support the development of formal speaking and provide students with support and opportunities to practice so that they can feel well-prepared.

- Teachers need to give explicit attention to the connections between speaking and listening.

- To foster active listening, teachers can encourage students to build upon one another's contributions to discussions or require them to write a brief summary of the discussion at the end of class.

NCTE Principles Regarding Language Instruction

A comprehensive statement of NCTE's principles on language instruction appears in "Learning through Language: A Call for Action in All Disciplines," which can be found on NCTE's website at http://www.ncte.org/positions/statements/learningthroughlang. It was prepared by NCTE's Language and Learning Across the Curriculum Committee.

Language is a primary way individuals communicate what they think and feel. They find self-identity through language, shape their knowledge and experiences by means of it, and depend on it as a lifelong resource for expressing their hopes and feelings. One of the goals of language instruction is to foster language awareness among students so that they will understand how language varies in a range of social and cultural settings; how people's attitudes toward language vary across culture, class, gender, and generation; how oral and written language affects listeners and readers; how conventions in language use reflect social-political-economic values; how the structure of language works; and how first and second languages are acquired. The CCSS provide standards for language instruction, but teachers should use their knowledge of language to help foster an interest in language that is contextually bound to other literate practices.

What we know about language and learning language:

- As human beings, we can put sentences together even as children—we can all *do* grammar.

- Students make errors in the process of learning, and as they learn about writing, they often make new errors, not necessarily fewer ones.

- Students benefit much more from learning a few grammar keys thoroughly than from trying to remember many terms and rules.

- Students find grammar most interesting when they apply it to authentic texts.

- Inexperienced writers find it difficult to make changes in the sentences that they have written.

- All native speakers of a language have more grammar in their heads than any grammar book will ever contain.

What this means for teachers of language:

- Teachers should foster an understanding of grammar and usage.

- Instructors must integrate language study into all areas of the English language arts.

- Teachers should experiment with different approaches to language instruction until they find the ones that work the best for them and their students.

- Teachers should show students how to apply grammar not only to their writing but also to their reading and to their other language arts activities.

- Teachers can make good use of the other languages and the various dialects of English in their classrooms.

- Teachers might try using texts of different kinds, such as newspapers and the students' own writing, as sources for grammar examples and exercises.

- Teachers should use grammar exercises that improve writing, such as sentence combining and model sentences.

NCTE Principles Regarding Teaching English Language Learners

The original version of this NCTE Guideline, entitled "NCTE Position Paper on the Role of English Teachers in Educating English Language Learners (ELLs)," can be found on NCTE's website at http://www.ncte.org/positions/statements /teacherseducatingell. It was originally authored by members of the ELL Task Force: Maria Brisk, Stephen Cary, Ana Christina DaSilva Iddings, Yu Ren Dong, Kathy Escamilla, Maria Franquiz, David Freeman, Yvonne Freeman, Paul Kei Matsuda, Christina Ortmeier-Hooper, David Schwarzer, Katie Van Sluys, Randy Bomer (EC Liaison), and Shari Bradley (Staff Liaison).

Multilingual students differ in various ways, including level of oral English proficiency, literacy ability in both the heritage language and English, and cultural background. English language learners born in the United States often develop conversational language abilities in English but lack academic language proficiency. Newcomers, on the other hand, need to develop both conversational and academic English. The creators of the CCSS note that the standards do not address the needs of English language learners (p. 6), but they also note that it is important for schools to consider and accommodate these students' needs while meeting the standards. These principles can provide a guide for teachers as they imagine what this might look like in their classrooms.

What we know about teaching multilingual learners:

- The academic language that students need in the different content areas differs.
- English language learners need three types of knowledge to become literate in a second language: the second language, literacy, and world knowledge.
- Second language acquisition is a gradual developmental process and is built on students' knowledge and skill in their native language.
- Bilingual students also need to learn to read and write effectively to succeed in school.
- Writing well in English is often the most difficult skill for English language learners to master.
- English language learners may not be familiar with terminology and routines often associated with writing instruction in the United States, including writing process, drafting, revision, editing, workshop, conference, audience, purpose, or genre.

What this means for teachers of multilingual students:

- For English language learners, teachers need to consider content objectives as well as English language development objectives.
- Because teachers relate to students both as learners and as children or adolescents, teachers must establish how they will address these two types of relationships, what they need to know about their students, and how they will acquire this knowledge.
- Teachers should provide authentic opportunities to use language in a nonthreatening environment.
- Teachers should encourage academic oral language in the various content areas.
- Teachers should give attention to the specific features of language students need to communicate in social as well as academic contexts.
- Teachers should include classroom reading materials that are culturally relevant.
- Teachers should ask families to read with students a version in the heritage language.
- Teachers should teach language features, such as text structure, vocabulary, and text- and sentence-level grammar, to facilitate comprehension of the text.
- Teachers should give students frequent meaningful opportunities for them to generate their own texts.
- Teachers should provide models of well-organized papers for the class.

NCTE Principles Regarding
21st Century Literacies

The original version of this Position Statement, titled "21st Century Curriculum and Assessment Framework," can be found on NCTE's website at http://www.ncte.org/positions/statements/21stcentframework. It was adopted by the NCTE executive committee on November 19, 2008.

Literacy has always been a collection of cultural and communicative practices shared among members of particular groups. These literacies—from reading online newspapers to participating in virtual classrooms—are multiple, dynamic, and malleable. Students need to be able to navigate the multiple literacy situations in which they will find themselves, and undoubtedly, they already engage with a number of literacies that were not available to their parents and teachers. The CCSS include standards for students' effective and critical use of technology, and the following principles can help teachers consider how to implement instruction that will empower students as technology continues to change and affect their literacies.

What we know about 21st century literacies and learning:

- As society and technology change, so does literacy.
- Because technology has increased the intensity and complexity of literate environments, the twenty-first century demands that a literate person possess a wide range of abilities and competencies, many literacies.
- Students in the twenty-first century need interpersonal skills to work collaboratively in both face-to-face and virtual environments to use and develop problem-solving skills.
- Students in the twenty-first century must be aware of the global nature of our world and be able to select, organize, and design information to be shared, understood, and distributed beyond their classrooms.
- Students in the twenty-first century must be able to take information from multiple places and in a variety of different formats, determine its reliability, and create new knowledge from that information.
- Students in the twenty-first century must be critical consumers and creators of multimedia texts.
- Students in the twenty-first century must understand and adhere to legal and ethical practices as they use resources and create information.

What this means for teachers of twenty-first-century learners:

- Students should use technology as a tool for communication, research, and creation of new works.

- Students should find relevant and reliable sources that meet their needs.

- Teachers should encourage students to take risks and try new things with tools available to them.

- Teachers should create situations and assignments in which students work in a group in ways that allow them to create new knowledge or to solve problems that can't be created or solved individually.

- Students should work in groups of members with diverse perspectives and areas of expertise.

- Students should be given opportunities to share and publish their work in a variety of ways.

- Teachers should help students analyze the credibility of information and its appropriateness in meeting their needs.

- Students should have the tools to critically evaluate their own and others' multimedia works.

NCTE Principles Regarding Assessment

The original version of this document, titled "Standards for the Assessment of Reading and Writing, Revised Edition (2009)," can be found on NCTE's website at http://www.ncte.org/standards/assessmentstandards. This document was authored by members of the Joint IRA–NCTE Task Force on Assessment, Peter Johnston (chair), Peter Afflerbach, Sandra Krist, Kathryn Mitchell Pierce, Elizabeth Spalding, Alfred W. Tatum, and Sheila W. Valencia.

Assessment is an integral part of instruction, and NCTE affirms its importance for student learning. In particular, formative assessment can be a powerful means of improving student achievement because it is assessment *for* learning, but it must adhere to key principles to be effective. These principles include emphasizing timely and task-focused feedback because it is feedback, not the absence of a grade, that characterizes effective formative assessment; shaping instructional decisions based on student performance in formative assessment; embedding formative assessment in instruction because the *use* of a given instrument of assessment, not the instrument itself, confers value on formative assessment; and offering students increased opportunities to understand their own learning. The principles below, developed in collaboration with the International Reading Association, suggest how assessment, both formative and summative, can enhance student achievement.

What we know about assessment:

- Assessment experiences at all levels, whether formative or summative, have consequences for students.
- Assessment should emphasize what students can do rather than what they cannot do.
- Assessment must provide useful information to inform and enable reflection.
- If any individual student's interests are not served by an assessment practice, regardless of whether it is intended for administration or decision making by an individual or by a group, then that practice is not valid for that student.
- The most productive and powerful assessments for students are likely to be the formative assessments that occur in the daily activities of the classroom.
- The teacher is the most important agent of assessment.
- Teachers need to feel safe to share, discuss, and critique their own work with others.
- Teacher knowledge cannot be replaced by standardized tests.
- The primary purpose of assessment is to improve teaching and learning.

What this means for teachers:

- Teachers should be able to demonstrate how their assessment practices benefit and do not harm individual students.
- Teachers must be aware of and deliberate about their roles as assessors.
- Teachers must have routines for systematic assessment to ensure that each student is benefiting optimally from instruction.
- Teacher leaders and administrators need to recognize that improving teachers' assessment expertise requires ongoing professional development, coaching, and access to professional learning communities. Nurturing such communities must be a priority for improving assessment.
- Teachers must take responsibility for making and sharing judgments about students' achievements and progress.
- Teachers should give students multiple opportunities to talk about their writing.
- Schools and teachers must develop a trusting relationship with the surrounding community.

Author

J eff **Williams** graduated from The Ohio State University in 1990 and has been a teacher of literacy in Ohio schools for more than 20 years. In 2001 he became the Literacy Teacher Leader for Solon Schools, where he has worked as a literacy coach, Reading Recovery Teacher, and staff developer for K–12 teachers. He was elected Assistant Chair of the Elementary Section of the National Council of Teachers of English (NCTE) in 2008 and served as a member of NCTE's Executive Committee from 2008–2011. He has chaired several NCTE committees, including the Government Relations Subcommittee, and headed the national NCTE Review Team providing feedback on the ELA Common Core State Standards. Williams is a regular speaker at national and state conferences, including NCTE's Annual Convention, the International Reading Association's Annual Convention, and the Reading Recovery Council of North America's National Conference, and provides literacy consulting in Ohio and many other states. He has coauthored several articles in *The Reading Teacher, Journal of Adolescent Literacy,* and the *Journal of Staff Development*. In 2011–12, he received the Hameray/Yuen Family Foundation Scholarship and has returned to Ohio State to pursue an intensive, yearlong Reading Recovery Teacher Leader training.

Contributing Authors

During her experiences as a high school and middle school teacher in rural Indiana, **Elizabeth C. Homan** grew dedicated to teaching underprivileged and struggling students in high-poverty communities. She earned her bachelor's degree from the University of Illinois in English with a secondary certification and went on to complete her master's degree at Purdue University while teaching in districts surrounding West Lafayette, Indiana. Interested in the potential of place-conscious education that meets the needs of students in rural communities, Homan presented at local and regional conferences during her master's work, as well as at the National Council of Teachers of English Annual Convention in 2009 and 2010. In addition to teaching high school and middle school students, she has tutored English language learners, taught preservice teachers, and taught first-year writing at Purdue University and The University of Michigan, where she is currently working on her PhD in English and education.

Sarah Swofford's interest in rural and underprivileged students began during her years teaching in rural middle and high schools in Texas and South Carolina. She also taught in a Middle College, where she explored co-teaching interdisciplinary courses. These experiences led to her interest in how southern students and teachers approach language in the classroom. Swofford earned her BA in English from Anderson University in South Carolina and completed her initial certification through an alternative certification program at Baylor University in Waco, Texas, where she completed an MS in education, curriculum, and instruction. In addition to teaching English language arts to middle and high school students, she has coaxed many students onto the stage for their first theatrical productions and enjoys teaching first-year writing at The University of Michigan, where she is currently pursuing a PhD in English and education.

This book was typeset in TheMix and Palatino by Precision Graphics.

The typeface used on the cover is Myriad Pro.

The book was printed on 60-lb. White Recycled Opaque Offset paper by Versa Press, Inc.

30% Total Recycled Fiber